SHRINK

BY

Dr. DAVID WOLGROCH

Copyright© 2006 David Wolgroch

Lulu Press

London, England

ISDN 978-1-84728-160-9

SHRINK

INTRODUCTION

It is not easy to be normal when you are a shrink. For me the problem began during the early stages of formal studies. Everyone seemed to depict worrying signs of unrecognised psychopathology, depending on whatever clinical syndrome was being studied at the time. Dad was showing signs of paranoia, mom was passive-aggressive, my girlfriend was acutely hysterical, and my wretched roommate, Tony, was exhibiting the early stages of drug induced schizophrenia with psychotic delusions of grandeur. I came out surprisingly normal, except for a brief period of acute panic after incorrectly interpreting the results of a self-assessed personality test, which indicated that I was a lesbian. Some go for therapy during their studies. I was relieved that I was not studying oncology.

The second challenge to sanity takes place during clinical supervision. Delving into someone else's subconscious can be quite perilous if you cannot separate the patient's pathology from your own. At least that was the rationale given for the relentless examination of my reactions to clinical material. "I noticed that you arrived late today," my supervisor would say, "Does this have anything to do with your difficulty in accepting authority?" As a rule, most clinical supervisors find it easier to interpret your comments rather than respond to them.

Then there is the daily exposure to severe maladjustment. The spectrum of psychopathology is as dynamic as it is challenging. For some, Human nature provides the creative impetus for music, art, and poetry. It is quite simply a job for the clinical psychologist. A similar process is experienced by policemen who adopt a dismal perception of the world that is based upon crime and punishment, or firemen who notice subtle safety infringements while out with the family for dinner. Fleeing from threat, danger, or bizarreness may be considered a natural reaction among normal people. But the clinical psychologist tries to engage, to confront, and to contain. In time one develops a defensive barrier, in the form of professionalism, which helps maintain the vital boundaries needed for self-preservation.

It is the banal, and sometimes ridiculous, reactions of others at cocktail parties that set the psychologist apart from normal people. "So, what am I thinking?" someone might challenge – assuming that I had the extrasensory powers of a telepathic medium. Or they might call a friend over and teasingly joke, "Here's someone you gotta meet. He needs a shrink." Over the years I have developed a fund of reactions to these embarrassing situations. There are funny responses, mischievous ones, and serious ones – depending on my mood. For instance, a not uncommon question is, "What is the difference between a psychologist and a psychiatrist?" to which I might say, "Oh, about 40 bucks an hour," if I wanted to be funny.

The question that I hate the most is, "So, what made you become a Shrink?" It is asked in the same manner that one might wonder why someone was a vegetarian. My response is either non-committal, evasive, or funny. Failing this I ask, "So, why is that question so important to you?" in a classical analytical tone of voice, as Freud would have responded. Invariably the topic is changed.

Don't get me wrong. I like being a Shrink. No day is like the previous one. The complexities of Human Nature continue to fascinate me. I get a great sense of satisfaction from managing to identify the underlying issues that drive people to behave illogically. Manoeuvring through the rigid defences of a paranoid schizophrenic can be as exciting as playing chess. Encouraging someone bent on suicide to re-engage in life is rewarding. Every day presents a new challenge.

Over the years I have managed to build up a robust private practice in a plush tree-lined suburban neighbourhood. My office has a large green leather sofa and matching armchair, where I usually sit. A tropical fish tank stands between two large windows that face the East. Books that line the walls are not just for show. A large flat screen computer monitor sits on my antique oak desk in a corner, which is lit with expensive china-based table lamps.

Looking around me I can understand why others consider me 'established'. Indeed, things worked out well, considering. Few would guess how far I had come. No one has any idea that my career began in the slums of the Bronx. What would they say if they knew about the gang life, the crime, and the poverty? They certainly won't understand why I did what I did, back in 1969, unless they heard the whole story.

I

The Bronx was nowhere to be in August 1969. Two months of relentless sun had forged the cement pavements into mosaic slabs of putrefied litter. The lack of a decent breeze meant that exhaust fumes lingered, and merged into an invisible carbon monoxide cloud - until eventually settling onto any exposed surface in the form of black soot. The natural colours of park foliage faded into an indistinguishable brownish/yellow landscape within which little solace was found from the humidity. Billboards were outdated, the graffiti was random, and schools remained idle.

Entire city blocks were totally deserted after desperate tenants torched their own homes in order to coerce the city into providing hotel accommodation. Most of the windows were securely boarded up with aluminium sheets. Large sections of chain link fences were unravelled in order to provide easy access into playgrounds, school basketball courts, and mid-street crossings over busy roads. Left behind was a collection of abandoned cars in various stages of disrepair, or abuse.

The unfortunates who were not able to escape the summer misery of the Bronx appeared stubbornly sluggish in their movements. Many wore simple attire, which consisted of DIY shorts made from old jeans, loose fitting T-shirts with the sleeves ripped off, and plastic flip-flop sandals. It was almost as if people remained in the casual, well worn clothing that one restricts to lazy Sunday afternoons at home. At first a quick dash to the local newsagent was chanced without dressing up. Soon a slightly longer excursion to the bakery on the next block would hardly be noticed. Eventually care about one's appearance was abandoned in favour of comfort.

We were among the thousands of fortunate urban families who regularly escaped the summer torment of the Bronx to the Catskill Mountains in upper New York State. Those summer months would comprise the happiest memories of my childhood. The country air was fresh, cool, and fragrant. Little time was spent in the meagre cabin at Weis' Bungalow Colony. Mostly we enjoyed swimming in the large concrete pool and playing baseball, hide-and-seek, checkers, and Frisbee.

The nearby woods provided plenty of adventure. Top-secret paths towards a hidden field of blueberry bushes were cleared. Hideouts were camouflaged, and wildlife was collected. Regular competitions were held to see who could amass the most orange-coloured salamanders, the fattest toads, and the creepiest Daddy-Long-Leg spiders.

Evenings began with a barbecued meal consisting of hamburgers, salad, and a baked potato. We would play cards or hitch a ride to the nearby town for a strawberry milkshake. At night we sneaked into the resort hotels in the area for a free movie, stage show, or game of 8-ball. Most importantly were the seasonal friends who would serve as annual milestones of our growing development.

I wished that the summer would never have to end. But there was school and Dad, who usually came up on weekends. Besides, the cooling climate left us in no doubt that we needed to head back home. The two-hour journey provided time to make the transition between sad separation blues and anxious anticipation of arriving home and beginning school. Upon approaching the outskirts of New York City, Sara barked, "OK, it is time! Shut all the windows!" Immediately Mike and I obliged by pressing as hard as we could on the switch for the electric windows of our new Country Squire Station Wagon. This was one of the few occasions that a manual window could have been better since a final tug on the handle would confirm that the window was hermetically sealed. Electric windows don't provide that satisfaction. Dad turned up the air conditioner to the 'Super Kool' setting. Tinted glass helped screen the hot sun.

We cautiously entered the Bronx as if driving into a war zone. Upon reaching home, Dad kept the air conditioner on for several minutes while we prepared for the daring exit. We counted down from 10, like a space launch, until simultaneously bursting out from the cool air filtered environment of the car into the disgusting Bronx air, which we were to breathe for the next ten months. The staunch, smelly, polluted air hit us like a brick wall. Of course we made sure to exaggerate our reaction by emitting loud retching sounds, demonstrative coughs, a slight buckling at the knees, and dramatic last gasps for air - until Mom ostracized us for making a public spectacle of ourselves.

The toxic Bronx air appeared normal by the time that our belongings were unpacked. We quickly settled into a regular routine at home. There was screamingly little to do until next week when school was to begin. Sara was going to college. Mike was beginning the 6th grade, and I would be entering the junior year at William Howard Taft High School, which was just around the block.

Evenings were most unsettling. Night provided little respite from the humidity. The concrete matrix emitted stored heat from the previous day's sun. Few private homes enjoyed air conditioning in the 1960's. The best we could do was to purchase an inexpensive water-cooled fan at Woolworth's, thinking that it was superior to a simple fan. Of course this device increased the level of humidity more than it decreased the room temperature. But psychologically it was all we had to convince us that some measure of relief was achieved. Our black and white television offered little distraction. Most evenings were spent hung awkwardly over an open window listening to the sounds of a restless city. I didn't dare venture into the dark Bronx jungle without my trusted German Shepard Dog.

It was at night that dubious characters emerged from their sinister perch seeking mischief, drugs, and easy prey. One could hear the soft rhythmic bongos of Latino gangs from the park across the street. It was as alluring as it was foreboding. It was on one of these evenings that Sara suggested that we go for a pizza.

Gino's Pizza Parlour was a short stroll away on 171st Street. His Authentic Italian Pizza was legendary. Gino's competitor was less popular - except for a brief price war when the cost of a pizza dropped to ten cents. For one dollar you could get a generous slice of pizza and a cold drink. Most importantly, Gino's was air-conditioned.

We found Gino's practically empty except for a group of Puerto Rican boys playing cards at a back table. I ordered my usual double slice of pizza and a cherry/coke with crushed ice in a cone-shaped paper cup. Of course, as every Bronxonian knows, the proper way to eat pizza is double-decked. We situated ourselves at a Formica-topped table directly across from the air conditioner – making sure to prolong our time at Gino's as much as possible.

Sara wondered why we didn't think to bring something to do to pass the time. Mike suggested that we play with make-believe cards. So we dealt an imaginary deck of cards with ridiculous rules and outrageous exclamations of victory, cheating, and dramatic losses. It was fun, for a while.

As I got up to pay Gino at the counter, the Puerto Rican boys suddenly marched outside making sure to brush up against my back as they passed. We hadn't noticed that they had become very quiet. The smaller one of the group lingered behind. He firmly tapped me on the shoulder and announced, "We call'n you out!"

"What's that?" I asked.

"You heard me, Man. Weez call'n you out!" he replied. This time he pointed to his friends outside of the shop. Awaiting me was a group of chain swinging, knife flashing, and very angry looking hoods. Gino immediately took action by taking my money and resolutely escorting us from his shop. "I don wan no trouble in my chop!" he warned in a surprisingly distinct Greek accent. The shop door was closed behind us, with the shade drawn. I knew that Gino wouldn't call the police. That is the way it was in the Bronx: Don't get involved; mind your own business.

We stood in the middle of the gang who had quickly encircled us. They taunted us with ominous gestures, threatening curses in Spanish, and sneering expressions. I knew to keep my cool, even though I was scared shitless. Before me was the quiet member of the bunch leisurely lying on the unfortunate hood of a parked Chevy. He was obviously the elder of the gang. He wore battle fatigues that were crudely ripped in strategic places. His tall figure slid effortlessly off of the hood, like a snake from its rock, to stand erect directly in front of me. With confident skill he orchestrated complete quiet by a subtle flick of a finger. He then took off his sunglasses and looked me right in the eye. I didn't flinch.

"You woof'n on us, Man!" he accused, with clenched teeth.

"What do you mean woofing?" I naively asked.

"You know....woof'n... You mak'n fun of us Jew Boy," he accused. My Jewish *Chai* necklace had given away more than I wanted. Unfortunately, for many in the Bronx it had become synonymous with easy prey. Jews were better known for their willingness to move out to the safe suburbs than for their readiness to fight. I hated that part of being Jewish.

No amount of explanation would convince them that our innocent card game was exactly that: an innocent game. We were to be taught a lesson. We were to learn respect for our Puerto Rican neighbours. In other words, we were going to get the ass kicked out of us. I was determined to find a way out of this situation without betraying my pride, or my physical health. Then the first lucky break occurred: one of the gang called him by his name.

"David?" I queried. "That is my name, too."

"Yeah, well fuck me!" he exclaimed. "I mean… fuck you," he quickly corrected himself. The others laughed - thinking that it was a purposeful joke. The tension was broken. I was not free but the door was in sight.

I suggested that the entire issue was an affair between Men: between David and David. Why not let my sister and young brother go. I will take whatever is coming to me, I suggested. Dave was impressed. He wasn't about to be manipulated out of punishing me, but the manly challenge could not be denied. He agreed to let my sister, Sara, go home.

Now here is a point for which I have a different memory of the event than my brother, Mike. He maintains that he remained with me, and that my sister went home, alone. I recall that only I remained with Dave and the gang. Perhaps my focus was on my efforts to deal with them. It is funny about the memory of events like these. It seems so easy to remember certain details, like the colour of the faded white Chevy, the metallic clang of chains, or Dave's crooked teeth. Other facets of this event, even some important ones, remain hazy. Mike is probably right about this but I will continue to relate the subsequent events in the way that my mind tells me to. My apologies to Mike, who has complained of being deleted from various memories in the past. We tease him about this.

Sara unhesitatingly left the scene with a flippant wave after asking if I would be OK. However it was not asked as a question but as a request for confirmation. "Oh yeah," I replied, in an unconvincing tone, "We'll work this out. No problem." I had hoped that Sara would see through my façade of confidence and immediately call for help as soon as she got around the corner. But Sara went home reassured that I would be arriving shortly after settling this simple misunderstanding.

The gang frog marched me through a dark maze of alleyways between burnt out high- rise apartment buildings. Our path was more like an obstacle course than a retreat. There were fences to climb, walls to leap over, garbage cans to jump, and assorted trash to kick aside. Dimly lit basement corridors, which smelled of incinerated ash, provided passage between apartment blocks. They were obviously well acquainted with this route. I struggled to keep up.

Eventually we arrived at an all-night laundromat only a few blocks away. It was vacant except for a weary Chinese woman absentmindedly folding linen in a back room. She didn't seem concerned – about anything.

Dave directed me to sit across from him straddled on a long wooden bench.

"D'ju know Dead Man's Alley?" he asked.

"Yeah…I've heard of it," I calmly replied. I was in fact well aware of the stories about Dead Man's Alley. It is where bodies were mysteriously found in the mornings with their skull cracked open – an urban legend, I had hoped.

"Yeah, well. We're gonna take your there, "he threatened.

The gang were overjoyed. I wondered why we stopped at this laundromat if that was the plan all along. Could it be that Dave was not so anxious to terminate this affair? He seemed to be enjoying this game, like a cat with its prey.

"Hey, Dave," I chanced, "I'm sure we can work something out."

"Shiit, man. We'll work YOU out, "he retorted. Again the gang showed appreciation of Dave's quick wit. I began to realise that my punishment was not his aim. Dave was using me to entertain his gang. I was their amusement.

Gaining courage I suggested that we play for my fate. "You're a gambling man. You're not afraid of risks. How about we play for it?" I ventured.

Dave surprisingly liked this idea. I was playing along. I was showing respect. A game of 'Nucks' was dealt, in similar manner to the presentation of weapons before a duel of honour. 'Nucks' is a uniquely Bronxonian game of cards, whose rules I have long forgotten. I can only recall its punishing end: the loser willingly receives raps on the knuckles - hence the name - using a full deck of cards. The more you lose, the more 'Nucks' you get. Only Dave had decided that I would receive punches instead of knuckle raps.

Normally I was pretty good at 'Nucks'. I might have actually won this game if it hadn't been for Dave's cronies, who looked over my shoulder and unashamedly whispered my cards to him in Spanish. Besides, beating Dave at 'Nucks' would not have gone down very well. Not surprisingly I lost by 68 points!

The time of reckoning had arrived. I had run out of ideas. They slammed me against a wall between the detergent dispenser and a pay phone while arguing over who gets to throw the first punishing blow. Dave didn't interfere. He seemed to enjoy the disorder.

Suddenly a new idea came to mind. "Hey, Dave, there has gotta be some way that I can prove myself to you. You are the leader, aren't you?" I had nothing to lose, I thought.

"No Bull Shiit, Man'" he confirmed.

I suggested a test of strength. Or maybe a daring challenge would work. Anything but punches would suffice. After conferring briefly with his 'cabinet' Dave decreed that I would be spared punches if I can do the assigned number of push-ups. "They have to be Marine style," he demanded. This meant that I would have to perform 68 push-ups in which I clap my two hands together in between each thrust from the floor. "You better do them right," he warned.

I was never much good at sports. In Gym class, black players monopolized the basketball courts after ensuring that their friends got chosen for the three on three teams. This typically left a small group of boys sitting along the benches until the period bell rang. We told jokes, watched basketball games, and, somehow, worked up a smelly sports uniform. This was the norm until Mr.Cunningham joined the P.E. staff. He was young, handsome, athletic, and an ace in gymnastics. We received expert training in the high bar, the parallel bars, the horse, and mat exercises. Thanks to Mr. Cunningham I was in better shape than usual. Besides, the adrenalin that must have been streaming through my stressed body gave me superhuman strength.

I breezed through the challenge in record time. I was as surprised as Dave was. "Shiit, Man," he exclaimed, "You are not half bad for a Jew boy." Then Dave made two decisions that would change my life. Firstly, he decided a reprieve: I would not have to endure any punches. The second decision, however, surprised me the most. Dave offered me a place in his gang. I had, in his eyes, proven my worth. I took it like a Man. I had shown respect. That evening I became the only known Jewish member of a Puerto Rican gang in the Bronx. What an honour!

We played cards for the remainder of the evening. I feigned delight. They walked me home. It wasn't safe out there, Dave advised. Now that I was one of them I got protection. No one would dare mess with me when they know I am with him, he promised.

I was relieved to finally reach the safety of home. I lay in bed feeling strangely pleased with myself. It could have ended up much differently. Thanks to my wit, perceptive attention to Dave's needs, and self-control - I was in the clear. My only regret was that Dave had escorted me home. He knew where I lived.

II

The worst thing about the following morning was not that I awoke in a ring of sweat with the bed sheets on the floor. The lingering smell of laundry detergent, muscle aches, and unquenchable thirst were easily remedied with a long, cold shower. I didn't even mind the discovery that my bus pass wallet had mysteriously gone missing. What bothered me the most was that I had no one to tell about my adventure. Most friends had yet to return from their respective holidays. Who will gasp at my dramatic claims of a close shave with death? What audience will applaud my quick thinking? How will I confirm my survival?

Nothing was revealed to my parents, who would have undoubtedly reprimanded me for "taking such risks with those animals out there." Or, even worse, they might have involved the police and complicated the entire affair. Besides, it was one of those things that I needed to handle on my own. At 16, I sought opportunities to prove my manhood. I needed to cope. I needed to get on with it.

Conveniently I decided that the escapade was over. Dave had gotten what he wanted: cheap entertainment to break the monotony of a bleak evening. At least that is what I believed until the door bell rang.

"There is this *Goy* (Gentile) at the door, David," announced my mom. "He says he is your friend?" she scornfully asked. Mom had not unlatched the security chain of the door. At first I saw no one. However across the street I could make out the familiar silhouette of Dave as he leaned against a parked car. He was alone.

"Bull Shiit, Man," is how Dave greeted me. This was Dave's favourite expression that he used when he had nothing else to say. He looked exactly as he did the previous evening. Dave was dressed in his green battle fatigues – complete with heavy black boots and a wrinkled combat vest.

"Bet y'wanna cool down, "he correctly guessed. "I know a place we can swim for free," Dave enticed.

"You're not going to swim in those clothes?" I asked.

"Bull Shiit, Man," explained Dave.

I began to wonder if Dave had any mothering at all. Anyway, I wanted to distance Dave from the home as quickly as possible before questions were asked. We walked the short distance to the nearest subway station on 161st Street. There the remainder of the gang were impatiently awaiting us. They were engaged in a spitting contest to see who could fling a glob of mucous the farthest. Spitting, it turned out, was a major pastime of Dave's gang. It had something to do with being tough.

The waist-high turnstiles at the entrance of the station were easily vaulted - in total disregard of the solitary worker who was helplessly enclosed in a glass ticket booth. He barely looked up. We hopped onto the last carriage of the first train to arrive at the station. Only momentarily did the passengers allow themselves to look up at us. Recognising trouble they quickly buried themselves into a newspaper, in ostrich-like fashion, as if to deny our presence. Purses were tightly held. After a brief period of silence Dave announced, "Bull Shiit, Man. It's boring in here!"

Dave led us in a frenzied game of follow-the-leader towards the front carriages of the train. We noisily rampaged through the train via connecting doors - swinging around centre poles, stomping on exposed feet, and simulating falls onto unsuspecting laps. At station stops we jumped on and off of the train making sure to dodge the hydraulic closure of the doors. I lagged somewhat behind struggling with the urge to apologise for the preceding insult. No one dared to intervene. Some uttered angry comments to their neighbour. I hoped that Dave had not overhead them.

Eventually we arrived at our destination: The East River. Large white rocks lined its bank. A disused wooden pier extended into the water. At the end of the pier dangled a long, thick rope with a large rubber tyre knotted to its end. We used this as a swing to bomb precariously close to submerged rocks in the river. It was more fun than chasing each other through the spray of illegally opened fire hydrants, or wading in a shallow pool of water after clogging up the drain of kiddy-park sprinklers. Mostly we splashed a lot.

But no one splashed Dave. He was no different in the water than on land. Dave immediately organised various competitions and challenges. He remained at the centre, and in complete control. Observing him from the pier I noticed a different picture altogether. He swam in an awkward fashion – making sure to keep his head above water. His strokes were more like dog paddles than confident expressions of mastery. Somehow he appeared vulnerable, like a frightened child desperate to subdue his anxiety. I suddenly realised that Dave was being supported by his gang and not vice-verse, as he would prefer us to believe. Their proximity and devoted attention to him gave Dave a sense of security. I began to feel less afraid of him. I began to wonder what role I played into Dave's frightening psyche. This intrigued me.

At breaks Dave and I collected smaller stones and sat along the pier. We targeted the large, black, hairy rats that scrambled for safety between the bank's rocks. Dave commented that I was a good shot. This pleased me. It was a sincere exchange without shows of bravado or expressions of power. I wondered if there was another, hidden, side of Dave that might be worthwhile discovering. Suddenly we noticed a strange man standing on the shore nearby. He was taking photographs of us.

"What the fuck!" erupted Dave. "What you look'n at?" he challenged. Dave clearly felt exposed.

"It's a free country, " provoked the photographer.

That was a big mistake! All hell broke loose. We chased him for several blocks until he was cornered in a blind alley. He offered his wallet, which Dave readily took. His watch went, as well. Then the camera was smashed to the ground. He might have explained why he was taking photographs of us if his jaw hadn't been broken. I realised how lucky I had been the night before. It would be quite awhile before Dave allowed himself to be sincere.

That weekend I discovered a series of photographs in the centre section of the Daily News. One of the pictures was captioned, "UNDERPRIVELEDGED YOUTH SWIMMING IN THE POLLUTED EAST RIVER TO COOL OFF." The photograph depicted all seven of us hanging in a row onto the rope. Dave was sitting within the tyre. No mention was made of the photographer's unfortunate encounter with us. I wondered if I was, indeed, underprivileged. It certainly didn't feel like that when we were swimming. It did now.

III

I was no more successful in denying the realities of the following day than I was in repressing the troubling dreams of the night before. Most of the morning was spent desperately trying to remain asleep. The predicament with Dave could no longer be seen as a transient affair that would resolve itself in time. On the contrary, my efforts to appease the gang – by pretending to enjoy their company – had strengthened their interest in me as a friend. This, I was not.

No doubt Dave would call for me sometime during the day. Perhaps I could find something to do away from home? Quite simply, I might be able to evade Dave until he tires of me. How would he react, I wondered? He will probably get mad. He might even get angry with Mom, or do something to the house – like, break the glass door. Then I would have to avoid him and the gang forever. On the other hand I could wait until he calls for me and say that I was busy. Could I find excuses for another five days until school starts? Would Dave fall for this? Or would he realise that I was avoiding him, and that my delight at being in the gang was fake? My mind raced in vain.

Eventually Mom relieved me of this dilemma by sending me to the local grocers for a pint of milk. I readily agreed, to her surprise. Thoughts about the gang were momentarily displaced by concerns about what type of milk to buy. How much money will I need? Was anything else needed? Perhaps it was best to avoid Mr. Castro's shop, our regular grocer. His shop was within Dave's territory. They might catch sight of me there. What would I say? Alas, the worries about the gang were back on my mind.

I decided to go to the competing grocer on 171st Street in order to see if any friends had returned from their holiday on the way. Then I could cut through the park, slip across the Grand Concourse, and pop into the grocers without being seen. I'll take a different route home just in case I was noticed. The whole mission would take less than 15 minutes, if I run.

My plan would have worked fine except for the inquisitive grocer who wondered why I don't shop there regularly.

"So, you live just around the corner on Morris Avenue, "he said. "Your Mom must go to Castro's, right?" he guessed.

"Oh, I am not sure. I think she goes to the big A & P supermarket on Jerome Avenue. I dunno… I am kind of in a hurry," I impatiently replied.

"Tell your Mom that Castro is a thief. She should watch his calculations," he warned.
The more annoyed I became, the less hurried he appeared.

"Yes, your shop is great! It is the most beautiful shop in the Bronx. We are fools for shopping anywhere else, and promise to do all of our purchases here for the rest of our lives," is what I was willing to say to get my 32 cents change and leave. What I wanted to say was, "Just give me the change, you asshole!"

My luck ran out with a sharp blow to the spine. "Hey, Jew," greeted Alex cheerfully as he slapped me hard on the back. Alex was the serious one of Dave's gang. His short stature made him very sensitive to criticism. Alex cared a lot about his appearance. He was constantly trimming his thin moustache, re arranging his collar, or checking for gum stuck on the soles of his black leather boots. We hardly spoke.

"*Que Passa?*" I replied.

Alex explained that Dave and the gang were wondering where I was. They had spent most of the day at the laundromat playing cards. He was sceptical about my excuse about being busy. Shopping for Mom was a girl's job, in Alex's eyes.

"So, what are YOU doing at the grocers?" I challenged.

"Bull Shiit, Man! I'm pick'n up some things for Mercedes' Sweet Sixteen party tonight, "he explained. Mercedes was Dave's girlfriend whom I have heard about. "We're meeting at eight," he said.

Alex had several six-packs of cheap beer, some potato chips, a few devil-dog cup cakes, and a bottle of fizzy wine in his arms. "I'm tak'n these," he announced to the grocer.

"Is this on the account?" nervously asked the grocer.

"Yeah, on account of *Tu Madre*," replied Alex, cynically.

"The milk, too?" asked the grocer looking at me.

Alex shoved me out of the door with the milk in hand. On the way out he grabbed a handful of bubble-gum. Before leaving Alex explained, "We don't pay for nothing in this shop. He owes us some favours, because Dave makes sure his place is safe. He should know better than to ask me for money. You, on the other hand, can pay." We went in opposite directions. I knew that Alex would not be a friend of mine. He resented Dave's interest in me. Of all the people to run into he was the worst. His report to Dave was unlikely to present me in a good light. I knew, now, that I had to show up for the party that evening.

I arrived at the laundromat shortly after 8 PM to find the gang still there, playing cards. Dave hardly showed interest upon my arrival other than to flash a brief smile at Alex, who looked distraught. We had a few rounds of 'Nucks' before leaving for the party. All of the items that Alex had lifted from the grocer were already depleted – meaning that we would arrive at the party empty handed.

I was surprised to see how easy it was for the gang to ride the bus for free. We, of course, boarded the bus through the rear exit as passengers got off. The driver hardly noticed our presence. It was, I assume, safer to tolerate minor transgressions than to risk confrontation. We got off at another forgotten neighbourhood of the Bronx near Crotona Park. There was something eerily familiar about this area. At first I couldn't place it. The playground, neighbourhood shops, the dark red brick, fire escapes, and the four-story apartment buildings were not completely foreign to me. The realisation came upon noticing a small cluster of rocks at the edge of the park. Children were scaling them as if they were mountains. Suddenly I recalled that I, too, used to climb these rocks as a child.

This neighbourhood was almost exclusively Jewish in the past. It is where my parents lived shortly after their arrival into the United States of America, from post-war Europe. It is where I collected hundreds of Bazooka bubblegum comics to exchange for a racoon tail. It is where we received a used three-seat sofa, as a gift, that was too big to fit into the apartment. This is where I had witnessed a car accident, cried after being splashed in the park's wading pool, and scraped my elbow on the sliding pond. It is where I grew up.

The neighbourhood was home to Dave, as well. As we walked towards the party venue I noticed that Dave was clearly well known here. Shop owners greeted him, old men lounging at the entrance to buildings saluted him, and kids skipping rope ran up to him. Crotona Park, it would seem, was in both our pasts. We were both undeniably American from immigrant families, brought up in the same neighbourhood, and heading for the same party. Logic would expect us to be natural friends. We were likely to have similar ideals and to lead comparable lives with parallel opportunities for the future. Nothing could be more wrong.

We climbed to the fourth floor of the building where the party was being held. The elevators were either inoperable or unreliable. The narrow concrete staircase was dimly lit and covered with flakes of grey paint from the peeling walls. Many doors were left open to permit the vital flow of air from an opened window. From the meagre apartments came loud aromatic smells of fried plantains and familiar sounds of the I Love Lucy Show or Latino music.

The ascent to the party was mostly uneventful, except for a brief encounter with a dope addict who was hallucinating on the stairs. He hardly reacted to the malicious kicks that the gang delivered, in turn, as they passed. Dave, I was told, had a particular hatred for druggies, drug pushers, and prostitutes ever since something horrible happened to his beloved sister, Maria. I didn't need further explanations.

It was easy to recognise the venue of Mercedes' party. People were spilling out of the door into the corridor. Loud, rhythmic Latino music shook the walls. Smoke filled the air. The atmosphere was jovial, exciting, and dynamic. Dave entered last in order to make a proper entrance. An attractive, longhaired girl with large ringed earrings immediately greeted him. She pounced onto Dave's back with her legs and arms wrapped securely around him. This, I assumed, was Mercedes.

Mercedes was a girl of little mystery. She dressed simply, never spoke - except through Dave - and remained under Dave's arm for the entire evening. The only thing that stood out about Mercedes was her big tits, which she unashamedly advertised.

No doubt that this gave her immense power in relationships with men. Other than this she didn't interest me, at all.

Others at the party welcomed me unreservedly after Dave introduced me as part of the gang. "He's a Jew, but now he is one of us," he decreed. I didn't know whether to apologise or to feel pride. It was best not to think too much about it, I thought. Besides, the party atmosphere was alluring.

Relieved I was to see the absence of hard drugs. I had wondered what to do if something was offered, or passed around. Hard drugs were definitely off limits, but marijuana intrigued me. Anxious schools and communities mobilized an army of police and experts to scare us away from drug use. We attended numerous lectures at school assembly during which we were handed graphically designed pamphlets warning us about the tragic consequences of drugs.

Specially commissioned films were screened in which the horrible effects of drugs were dramatised. One movie depicted a typical teenager seduced into taking a solitary whiff of marijuana. His eyes suddenly bulged from their sockets, his hair stood on end, and his clothes mysteriously became dishevelled like a werewolf at full moon. This crazed dope fiend then became madly aggressive towards the girls around him. Fortunately, for them, he impulsively threw himself out of the window – obviously thinking that he was a bird.

The film instantly became a hit with regular pot users, who watched it stoned. I think it was called, *Reefer Madness,* or was this the title of a movie by the popular comedy duo of Cheech and Chong, who played two stoned idiots stumbling through various escapades? These misguided documentary scare tactics and popular comedy spoofs became indistinguishable in time. Indeed, it didn't take a rocket scientist to realise that we were being duped. Friends who were known to be potheads were anything but depraved. Most were popular, good students, and, most importantly, cool. The more effort expended in educating us about drugs the more curious we became.

At any case drugs were unavailable due to Dave's adamant resistance to anything having to do with them. I did, however, get turned on to the fabulous music of Carlos Santana. More importantly, that evening was my first wonderful experience of French kissing. It was a far cry from the parties that I was accustomed to. There were no silly party games or embarrassing spin-the-bottle blushes. Supervising parents were not hiding in an adjacent room. This was much more grown-up.

We left the party together as we had arrived. The drug addict was still where we had last seen him. For some reason he was barking like a dog. Dave spat at him.

"So, you like Santana?" asked Dave

"Yeah, I gotta get his album, "I confirmed.

"Tomorrow, we'll get you one," he promised.

Despite my reservations, I had had a great time with Dave and his friends. Mercedes said that I could come again. Someone called *Chika* said I was a good kisser. I actually looked forward to tomorrow.

IV

There are two ways to travel by bus: the boring way, and the 'white-knuckled' way. Impatient shoppers, who had inconsiderately opted to catch an early bus rather than a timely shower, jammed into most of the buses. Dave, Alex and I leaped on to the back bumper while desperately holding on to the rim of the rear window with our fingertips. The others followed suit on a nearby bus.

The two buses sped down the twelve-lane Grand Concourse – over passing each other at alternate stops. We decided that it was a race to our destination: Fordham Road. Like two Roman chariots the vehicles vied for the lead. At times they travelled in parallel fashion as if threatening to ram the other into imaginary spectator stands. The roar of busy traffic became cheers of encouragement by a bloodthirsty crowd. The relentless pounding of motor pistons was likened to the powerful gallop of a team of horses. Occasional potholes in the road caused the bus to jerk, as if running over unfortunate gladiators who had fallen off their warring chariot. Dave commented that he wished he had a horsewhip, like Charlton Heston in the movie *Ben Hur*.

We taunted the others on the competing bus. They, in turn, spat on us. We retaliated by throwing loose objects at them in order to loosen their tenuous grasp. No one seemed particularly concerned about the tragic consequence of falling under the tyres of oncoming traffic. I guess that we hadn't thought this precarious game through to the end.

Suddenly I noticed that the route number of the second bus was different than ours.

"Hey, Dave," I shouted, "They are on the wrong bus. Theirs will turn off towards Ogden Avenue. We are going to win for sure!"

"Shiit, Man!" exclaimed Dave, "Those Fuckers!"

Knowing that our victory was ensured, Dave challenged the others to a dare. Whoever arrives last will be 'the runners', he decreed.

"Runners?" I asked.

"Yeah, you'll see," replied Dave.

As predicted the competing bus turned into a side road shortly before reaching Fordham Station. We laughed and jeered as they hopped off the moving bus and ran after us in vain. Upon arriving Dave put his left arm around my shoulder. He pulled Alex close to him with his right arm. We stood proudly, side by side, to welcome our breathless and defeated friends. I knew, now, that my status in the gang was ensured.

Fordham Road was a busy shopping district in the Bronx before the proliferation of shopping malls. It was the height of the seasonal sales. The sidewalks were buzzing with anxious shoppers hoping to grab a good bargain. Among them was an army of blue-haired pensioners pulling two-wheeled shopping carts with squeaky wheels. Barking dogs protested at being leashed to rusting signposts as their owners were in the shops. No one seemed to watch where he or she was going.

Our first stop was a popular Head Shop that sold all sorts of alluring paraphernalia related to drugs, rock music, and hippy fashion. I tried on a pair of flat leather sandals and stumbled around the shop wearing cool crystal spectacles that multiplied everything by twelve. One glass cabinet contained colourfully decorated smoking pipes and 'roach-clips' that were used to smoke the remaining morsel of a joint without burning the fingers. Another display presented an assortment of aromatic rolling papers and sculpted cigarette lighters. A sweet smelling incense stick burned in the corner beneath a black light that illuminated psychedelic posters of Bob Dylan, the Beatles, and Jefferson Airplane. Oversized speakers vibrated loudly to the sounds of sitar and bongo rhythms. Just about everything for the regular pothead was for sale, except the drugs.

Some guy tapped me on the shoulder while I was sifting through a collection of second hand Moody Blues record albums. He was a typical hippy - complete with the purple bell-bottomed jeans, the obligatory peace button, a skull shaped ring on his thumb, and long blonde hair. He smelled of Alfalfa.

"Hey, Man," he whispered, "D'ju know where I can score some grass?"

Overhearing this, Dave intervened and stood between us. "You got ten bucks?" he asked.

The deal was to be completed outside of the shop after Dave had received his money. For security reasons the stash of marijuana was to be hidden under a public telephone around the corner. That way no one could identify the transaction in case we were being watched. I was surprised that Dave was ready to deal in drugs despite his hatred for them. Indeed, the only thing to be found under the public telephone was a small bag of Oregano. What was this poor idiot going to do? He certainly won't go to the police.

Dave treated us to a meal at MacDonald's with the money. Soon Mercedes joined us. She was alone. We headed for the big Alexander's Department Store that boasted an expansive record selection. Dave and Mercedes asked to preview an album at the counter. They shared the same headphones while loudly singing to the music that only they could hear. All of the men in the department had eyes on Mercedes as she seductively danced next to Dave.

Alex suddenly shoved a record into my hands. "Here's your Santana album, "he begrudgingly announced. "Hold on to this until we take care of it. Just keep your eyes on us, "he directed. Shortly afterwards I heard shouts of the security guard as he chased the others out of the shop. I ran after the commotion easily overcoming the weighty guard who seemed more intent on giving the impression of chasing us than on actually catching us. Anyway, he gave up before reaching the curb. In a secluded back alley, several blocks away, a stash of 24 record albums was accumulated. Dave and Mercedes arrived shortly afterwards to assess the catch.

The gang rejected most of the albums. Someone had randomly grabbed a bunch of albums that were displayed within the '**M: Various Artists**' category. Barry Manilow and Mitch Miller were unceremoniously flung, like flying saucers, into a brick wall. Henri Mancini suffered a similar fate. I unashamedly stood quietly by while Mozart smashed into a parked car. But when Van Morrison's turn arrived I grabbed Alex's cocked arm.

"What a waste!" I exclaimed. "Why throw these away when we can sell them to the Head Shop?" I suggested. Dave liked this idea. "You see, that is why Jews is rich," he explained. I wished that I had not said anything. Someone standing behind me jeered "Watch the Jew! He'll steal the money." Instinctively I twisted around and sharply elbowed him in the nose. He was grounded. His head bounced off the pavement. Blood oozed from the nose.

I was paralyzed with concern over how Dave and the gang would react. I had, after all, knocked down one of the gang, who happened to be Dave's cousin. At any moment I expected to be pounced upon by the gang. All looked towards Dave for an indication of his response. Dave looked down upon his unfortunate cousin, who by now was sobbing like a baby. He was pleading for mercy.

"Shut up! Man, shut up you pussy!" demanded Dave. "Stop crying like a whimp you piece of shit!" he added with revulsion in his eyes. Dave bent down over his frightened cousin and slapped him in the face. A vicious assault followed in which Dave delivered relentless blows on the head, kicks to the groin, and a final spit in the eyes. Dave was livid with disgust and anger at the cries for compassion. He loathed weakness.

Dave approached me and slapped me hard on the head. "That's how you do it," he explained. "Don't ever do that again," he warned. I wasn't sure if Dave meant the assault on his cousin, or my reluctance to follow through to the end. I was afraid to ask.

No attention, whatsoever, was given to the unfortunate cousin, who followed us towards the Head Shop. He stuffed tissues in the nostrils to stop the bleeding and rubbed the back of his head. Everyone avoided direct eye contact with him. Dave handed me the collection of stolen record albums before reaching the shop. I was directed to execute the transaction in order to minimize suspicion.

The shop owner took me behind beaded curtains into a back storage room. Dave stood quietly behind me while the remainder of the gang carelessly examined items in the shop, as a distraction. The owner offered $1 per album that was not damaged. Classical albums were worth only 50 cents. He meticulously examined each album for scratches by slipping the record out of its sleeve and holding it against the desk lamp. One by one the albums were put in a pile on the desk as a tally was called out. Dave discreetly handed me an extra album that was omitted in the original pile. Shortly afterwards yet another omitted record was handed to me. Looking behind me I noticed that the gang had been selecting used albums that were on sale in the shop and slipping them to Dave. The naïve shop owner was unaware that he was, in effect, buying his own albums. Our original stash of 18 record albums quickly turned into 28 bucks, which was shared between the gang. I got the Santana album that was promised to me.

I played the record over and over again until able to accurately predict the track sequence, as well as the inevitable scratches that developed on its soft, vinyl surface. Somehow this comforted me. Alas, a similar sense of mastery over the troubling events of the day proved more elusive. These, too, spun relentlessly in my mind.

Dave's explosive reaction to his unfortunate cousin confounded me the most. I might have expected him to comfort his wounded friend. It wouldn't have surprised me if Dave had egged him on to get up and fight me back. Even some punitive punches directed at me might have been logical, albeit painful. But Dave didn't do any of these things. Instead his cousin was beaten mercilessly. No words of encouragement were heard. No help was offered.

Within an instant Dave's beloved cousin had been cruelly abandoned. He was ousted from the protective circle of good friendship into the dark and damned world of estrangement – like a piece of rancid flesh to be discarded. There was, apparently, no grey area in Dave's world. You were good or evil, worthy or dirt, friend or enemy.

The other thing that I began to notice about Dave was his absolute hatred for weakness in people. Dave's world seemed to be divided into those who step on others and those who are trod upon. Victims "deserved what they got" according to Dave. Revealing signs of weakness in character was likely to evoke an extreme reaction in Dave. It was as if he was confronted with a subdued, hidden part of himself that he desperately struggled to deny.

Some things began to fall into place: the brief glimpse of vulnerability as Dave swam in the East River; Dave's extreme reactions to perceived insult; his intense anger towards the photographer and his cousin; and Dave's insatiable need for attention. I didn't quite know how to make sense of these observations, just yet, but my survival in Dave's twisted perception of the world depended on putting this all together. For now I realised that I needed to demonstrate absolute strength towards others while carefully avoiding the same towards Dave.

Dave was like a wounded lion with a thorn embedded in his paw. Approaching him would be an extremely tricky affair. However, failure to negotiate Dave's psyche was unthinkable. It meant either total inclusion into Dave's doomed way of life, or physical harm. This was to be my challenge. From now, I decided, I will focus on understanding what makes Dave tick.

V

Just what did William Howard Taft do wrong to have a high school in the Bronx named after him? He was, after all, the 27th president of the United States of America between 1908 and 1913. He may have achieved notoriety for creating thousands of jobs by expanding the civil service if he hadn't ruined it by amending the constitution to allow the government to tax incomes in order to pay for this. Similarly Taft tirelessly encouraged countries in conflict to seek arbitration, which was a novel idea at that time, in order to prevent war. He promoted the establishment of The League of Nations, alas, too late to prevent the Great World War.

Perhaps Taft's enduring legacy was cruelly attained by his untoward achievement of being the fattest president ever. Taft was so obese that he got stuck in his own bathtub in the White House on several embarrassing occasions. His own mother called him '*my pudgy wudgy boy*' – in public. The other thing that stood out about Taft was his legendary inclination to fall asleep in any circumstance: meetings, state dinners, and political rallies. This, certainly, didn't win him many loyal friends when it came time to name public buildings. The committee charged with this task honoured Taft with a street in Manilla, The Philippines, and my high school.

Taft's gargantuan chest might have momentarily heaved with pride upon seeing his name undeniably chiselled in stone above the impressive main entrance to the school. The grand, white, four-story building that took up two entire city blocks was encircled by a wrought iron fence, for the most part. Within its perimeter were a full dirt running track and an assortment of chain-netted basketball hoops anchored securely onto the edifice. Ninety-six steps led to a large entrance foyer, where Taft's portrait was fixed, somewhat ominously, between two large American flags. Below the painting stood a glass cabinet that displayed an impressive collection of school awards and honours. Indeed, Taft High proudly achieved its expected quota of sports trophies and community awards until 1963, after which the few subsequent achievements were sparsely arranged in order to fill the shelf.

Sara, who had attended Taft just prior to my admission, recalled a different school altogether from what I was to experience. During her attendance at Taft the students, and indeed most of the teachers, were white and middle-class. The clean-shaven, crew cut, square-faced principal, Mr.Linville, enforced a strict code of behaviour and rigid academic demands during his tenure. The 60's however were charged with a general assault on conventional rules if not the need for them altogether. Hence, the 'establishment' launched a futile defensive strategy before conceding unconditional defeat.

While society was experiencing a radical cultural upheaval Taft struggled to maintain a bubble of unflinching adherence to random directives about dress, behaviour, and allegiance to the contrite wisdom of previous generations. On one occasion Sara had been sent home from school for daring to appear in a mini-skirt. It was called a 'cool-lot' and was cleverly designed to look like a pair of shorts, or was it the other way around. Similar infringements in hair length, political badges, and rebellious variations of speech were met with fierce admonishment, as if challenging the basic moral fabric upon which society was built.

Life in the 60's was as dynamic and unsettling as vigorously stirring a long-standing stew in which essential ingredients had been suppressed to the bottom of the pot – close to the heat. A brisk swish of the ladle, which took the form of civil unrest, brought undervalued flavours momentarily to the surface. A subsequent stir reinforced the new social integration to provide full flavour in each enriching spoonful.

Students from predominantly underprivileged neighbourhoods were bussed to Taft High School in order to undo chronic disparity in educational resources. As Black and Hispanic families moved closer to the school some white middle-class families, followed by a handful of experienced teachers, frantically moved out into the suburbs before house prices plummeted.

Our neighbourhood was radically transformed within a short period of time. I soon found myself a minority in my own community, which taught me what it must have been like for many non-white minorities to feel alien in their own world. Some said this was reverse discrimination, others maintained that it was long overdue. I said, "Dave, it is up to you, alone."

In school the traditional annual prom became 'the soul dance'. Some Black students rejected demands to study French, German, and Spanish in favour of more culturally relevant classes in Swahilian – in much the same way that previous generations argued that Latin and Greek were obsolete. A policeman patrolled each floor, essentially to protect the teachers. There were rumours about a crack S.W.A.T. team on the roof with high-powered telescopes.

All rules were challenged, modified, and, sometimes, flatly abandoned. Grammar was no longer considered necessary in English class. It could be inferred quite naturally by encouraging an appreciation of literature and poetry, said the contemporary experts. Besides, grammatical rules, it was maintained, served to restrict creativity more than to provide guidance. My English teacher, Miss Bush, nervously abandoned her established teaching plan that included Shakespeare, Milton, and Hemmingway in favour of unrecognised Afro-American authors, obscure comments on contemporary issues facing the modern subway commuter, and experimental theatre.

One memorable class trip brought us to The Public Theatre, in the Village. The audience sat around a centre stage that was designed as a one-bedroom apartment without walls. A family of actors quite simply lived their normal lives on stage for us to observe and comment upon like fee-paying voyeurs. Microphones, which were available for the audience, provided the opportunity to communicate with the cast.

Occasionally someone would approach a microphone to ask," What were you thinking of when the dinner was overcooked?" or, "Did you realise that your nudity embarrasses the children?" Similarly, members of the cast might spontaneously approach the microphone to share a sudden brilliance in philosophical wisdom, such as, "Peace is only a word - war is real." What a joke, I thought.

We were permitted to read anything that met our fancy as long as it was published. I, of course, chose the shortest books possible. Poems, which were read before the class, were equally brief if not funny. I picked a poem that contained no words. It was about rain. It went like this,

> *Whoosh, whish, splat.*
> *Tish, zip, drizzle.*
> *Boom, crackle, and crack.*
> *Splash, splish, tizzle.*
> and so on for twelve pages!

The final exam, in English, required a personal composition. This was my Haiku:

> *Hang on leaf, hang on*
> *For life is nearly gone*
> *Yet, the gusts of wind*
> *Blow stronger.*

Similar compromises were conceded in Social Studies and History. At school, boys were compelled to learn 'Home Economics', which meant sewing and cooking. I learned to cross-stitch, double-stitch, and bake bread. Girls, in turn, attended carpentry, electricity and printing workshops. Dress codes were abolished in order to respect requests to don traditional African robes. Similar concessions were made in regards to popular trends in boys' hair length, which went over the ears; peace now buttons; and bare knees.

As an honour student I was a member of the elite Arista Society. We were ceremoniously presented with a special badge, which we were obliged to wear every day in order to serve as role models to other students. However, the pin quickly became a magnet for scornful remarks, and, sometimes, humiliating gestures. I wore my pin below the hem of my shirt pocket, well hidden behind a clever camouflage of selected Bic pens.

For a 16 year-old it was as exciting as it was overwhelming. I searched for elusive role models in a world that endeavoured to discredit them. For a time I tried to become a sports fanatic but could never appreciate the inherent value of memorising the R.B.I. and H.R. statistics of baseball players. Perhaps some form of social recognition could be achieved by becoming a dope fiend? I stumbled through the school hallway one day as if stoned on drugs, which only resulted in attracting sceptical frowns of fellow students. I joined the drama club and was cast in the major role of Andre Carnes in the hit musical, Oklahoma. Belonging to this unique group of extroverts was fun until the play director suggested that I say my lines, instead of singing them. "My character is an old man and doesn't have to sing", he explained. I knew what he really meant.

Next I tried becoming a marine biologist, like Jacques Cousteau, until someone turned my biology project, a Sea Anemone, into a makeshift pencil holder. Some measure of success was achieved by acting the class clown but this was hard work. In short, growing up in the 1960's felt like I was floating down a fast flowing stream with nothing to hold on to except my own balls. I never let go.

VI

The first day of school finally arrived. I searched desperately for my usual friends, but it was a big school. So big, in fact, that the students were assigned to an early or late session. Suddenly out of the corner of my eye I noticed my old friend, Charles Wood, at school. He was Black. Chuck, as I called him, was my absolute best friend in sixth grade. We did everything together. Chuck and I shared a common admiration of certain comic book heroes. We raced precariously down hilly streets on a skateboard, and pumped the swings high above the top bar in the park playground. On one autumn afternoon, Chuck and I were energetically pumping on the swings while singing the words to the new hit Beatles single, *Hey Jude*, at the top of our lungs. A Jewish woman nearby accused us of being anti-Semitic.

"Why are you yelling *Hey Jew*?" she complained.

"It's Hey Jude, not Hey Jew, and I am not anti-Semitic," I contested. "How can I be? I myself am Jewish," I explained.

Chuck said, "Hey, I didn't know you are a Jew."

"And, I didn't know you were black," I replied. We laughed and went on singing.

Our friendship in sixth grade was forged largely by chance. We were invariably seated together in the back row of the class, since both our surnames began with 'WO'. He went to a different Junior High School than I did. Upon noticing him I excitedly called his name. He didn't reply. I ran up to him and pulled at his colourful African robe to turn him around.

"Hey, Chuck!" I said. "It is me, David from sixth grade."

Chuck angrily grabbed me by the collar and pinned me against the wall. "I am not who you think I am! Now, I am M'Jumbo. Don't ever touch me again!" Those were the last words between M'Jumbo and me. He lunched with his friends; sat at the back of class; refused, on principle, to participate in class discussions; and avoided my occasional glance.

At lunch period I met most of my usual friends. I told them about my adventures, but they were not particularly impressed – except for the part about the French kissing. They, too, had stories to share. Scott had set up a new tropical fish tank with his dad. They travelled all the way to Pennsylvania to purchase a rare breed of Angelfish. Ronnie was so successful in baseball camp that he was offered a try-out for the minor leagues. Mark went to Mexico with his family. There, he was tempted by a prostitute that was as old as him mom – yuch! And Gary, who lived several houses from me, got yet another new English Racer bicycle. It was to replace the previous one that was stolen. The previous bike was a replacement for the one before that, also stolen. In fact, Gary had barely managed to break in new bicycles before local hoods accosted him. "You are such a putz!" I would say.

There was something about Gary that screamed, "PLEASE, ROB ME!" Once, while playing stickball, we were approached by three black kids who lived down the block.

"Hey, man! New coat?" they asked.

"Yeah, it is made of real leather," replied Gary, naively.

"Can I try it on?" they asked.

What happened next was obvious to everyone, but Gary. "No matter," explained Gary. "My father will get me another one. We are moving to Florida, anyway," he would say. Gary had been threatening to move to Florida ever since we moved into the area, eight years ago. His parents, who ran a child day care nursery on the ground floor of their home, could not bring themselves to choose family welfare over easy profits. "Just one more year," they would promise.

Meanwhile Gary's home was packed with all sorts of expensive stuff. They had wall-to-wall plush carpeting, a quality stereo system, central air conditioning, a maid, and the first real colour television set in the neighbourhood – instead of the ridiculous fake colour television in which a translucent plastic film that had four horizontal coloured stripes was stuck on to the black and white screen. This meant that heads were blue, the body was red, the legs were yellow, and feet were green.

The first week of eleventh grade helped clear my mind of Dave and the gang. I divided my notebook into five categories for each class. A seat near the window was claimed in Art class – from which several jars of colourful paint were mysteriously dropped to create an abstract masterpiece on the cement ground of staff parking space number 12. The beautiful Nadine opted to sit next to be in biology lab. I joined the drama club and registered for the photography interest group. We took advantage of the first lesson in the printing workshop to mischievously produce seasonal passes to the school swimming pool. Of course Taft High had no pool, but new freshmen didn't know that. Tickets were sold for one dollar. "Yeah, just follow the signs to the boys' locker room in the basement. Go out the field exit and you will find the pool," they were directed. When they complained, we unapologetically explained that the same was done to us, and that they can do the same to entering freshmen next year.

I was beginning to get used to the routine of early morning rushes and school dashes. Unfortunately I was not alone. Alas, Dave was waiting for me along my usual route to school on Monday morning.

"Bull Shiit, Man," he greeted. "So, you go to 'Tuffed', which was a common derivative of Taft that inferred something about its tough reputation.

We exchanged some brief social niceties before I could excuse myself in order to get to school on time.

"Yeah, let's go," announced Dave. "You are gonna need my protection in that school," he advised.

"But, you don't go to school. They won't let you in without a pass," I warned - hoping that he would abandon the idea. Dave, however, was not deterred. He claimed to have a pass. Sure enough no one questioned Dave at the gates. We passed a security guard; two teachers, assigned to watch the entrance; and one police dog that sniffed for drugs. Finally a school monitor asked for his identification at the door.

"Here's my I.D.," announced Dave provocatively as he punched the air with his fist, stopping inches from the monitor's nose. Surprisingly Dave had an alumni class ring on his finger, which regretfully allowed Dave to pass.

"Where did you get a class ring?" I asked.

"You don't wanna know," he replied.

Dave religiously escorted me to most of my classes that day. Not a single teacher questioned his attendance, not a one! Dave stood at the back of class during the lessons with his arms folded. He remained alertly silent. At lunch Dave cleared off a table that was near the window. No one joined us. I offered to share my packed lunch that consisted of a tuna fish sandwich on rye, potato chips, an apple, and a soft drink. But Dave had other ideas. He stalked behind other students who were eating their lunch and peered over their shoulders. Occasionally, when something caught his fancy, Dave courteously asked for a bite, which was usually granted. Upon finding something that tasted good enough Dave simply said, "Thanks," and walked away. One student nervously protested. So Dave took the sandwich of whoever was sitting nearby and put it on his plate. "You happy now?" he angrily announced. Needless to say, neither Dave, nor I, was particularly popular during lunch break.

After several days Dave tired of standing in class. He promised to be around in case of need. I had no idea where Dave went during his absences and didn't really want to know. We routinely met for lunch and on occasion Dave attended the beginning of class, as if to assert his self-appointed right to be there.

Perhaps, I hoped, Dave was secretly interested in going back to school. I could quite easily rekindle his desire for an education. Surely he would excel in Spanish class. But I was wrong. Spanish in Dave's mind was stolen from the Puerto Ricans who had founded Spain. He protested at the teacher's emphasis on Spanish history that did not provide equal respect to Puerto Rico.

I was no more successful in enlightening Dave about the metabolism of Paramecium, the women's suffrage movement, or the curious fact that all things fall to the ground at the same time regardless of weight. Poetry was certainly out of the question. Despair was finally realised after an unfortunate incident during my voluntary tutoring period with blind students.

The students needed help in piecing together ambiguities in taped lessons. Some had a particularly difficult time comprehending three-dimensional axes in geometry. But mostly my time was spent explaining developments in popular television soap operas that were, also, taped. "What is he doing, now," they might ask, "Were they kissing?"

They, like us, squandered most of their lessons on jokes, gossip, and horsing around. During the tutoring lesson, which Dave attended, a minor row broke out between two blind students. One chased the other around the wooden desk that was at the centre of the room. Dave was astounded by their ability to run blindly around the room. They must have the room memorised, he guessed. To test his theory Dave silently pulled a chair away from the table and into their path. I was too late to intervene. Laughing, Dave excitedly remarked, "See, these fuckers are cheating. They got everything memorised."

Up until now I was ambivalent about Dave. I was curious about him, but chiefly I feared him. His lifestyle left me excited, yet, apprehensive. But after this incident Dave evoked a new reaction in me. It frightened me almost as much as it motivated me. I knew that I had to do something about Dave and didn't care, much, how I did it.

VII

I left school using a different exit each afternoon in order to evade Dave. The following day I explained that my mom was ill, or that I simply did not see him. Claiming that I was detained in school for misbehaviour was his favourite excuse. But, eventually, Dave became suspicious. He expected absolute loyalty to the gang who were obediently waiting at the Laundromat.

"Don't let school ruin what is really important," he angrily warned. I pointed out that Mark Twain had said something similar about not letting learning affect his education. But Dave was not impressed. He thought I was accusing him of stealing someone else's idea. With Dave I needed to keep conversations simple. He demanded loyalty to his gang and to himself. It was an important issue for him. Paramount, perhaps.

Every afternoon we met the others at the usual spot to squander most of the day playing cards. Those that went to school arrived with their rucksacks, which had hardly been opened during the day. More effort had been expended in decorative graffiti than on the pages within. No one seemed concerned about homework, revising for exams, or coming home for dinner. To them, school was an obligation to be tolerated in order to meet up with the gang at the end of the day. To me it was the other way around.

Only Carlos remained apart from the group. He sat at the counter that was normally used to fold clothes doing math exercises. Carlos explained that it was better here at the Laundromat than at home. There he would have to share a small table in the kitchen with his two younger sisters. The table was cluttered with kitchen appliances and stained with crayon marks and sticky paste. His mother, who prepared dinner in their small kitchen, invariably had something urgent for him to do – like, carry the trash to the incinerator down the hall. Carlos' older sister had just purchased a new portable cassette player, which she insisted on playing at full volume. She could scratch like a tiger when challenged. The worst was his Dad who came home drunk after gulping several canned beers with his friends at the local *Bodega*. At times he was angry, even violent. He was less than helpful.

"Why are you wasting your time on those books?" he would charge. "At your age I was working hard at the factory," he challenged. "*Mucho Trabajo: Poco Dinero*," was his favourite expression.

"What's it like in your home?" Carlos asked.

"It is the same," I replied, making sure not to blink.

When Alex called Carlos to join the game, I said, "It's Okay, I'll take his place."

Carlos was permitted to continue his schoolwork unhampered as long as he remained with the gang. He was, in effect, demonstrating allegiance to them. Could this be the key to managing Dave? Was it fidelity that he demanded? How could I distance myself from Dave without appearing disloyal? My mind raced.

The perfect opportunity to test my hypothesis arose in the most unlikely place for this drama to unfold: the synagogue. Dad took me to the evening prayers for Rosh Hashanah, the Jewish New Year, at the Mount Sinai *Shul* near home. Prayer attendance had gradually waned to a bi-annual obligation ever since completing Bar Mitzvah studies there three years ago. Mostly I feared meeting Miss Bitter, my old Hebrew teacher, at services. She had this annoying habit of pinching my left cheek when I misbehaved in class. The right cheek was similarly twisted when she was proud of me. There was no winning. She pinched hard for an old spinster.

The synagogue was predictably packed with infrequent prayer shawls that suffered few signs of wear. Dad and I found a vacant seat near the back so that we could flip frantically through the pages to keep up with the service. Somewhere between my second and third yawn an unfamiliar noise was heard. There was shouting. Heads turned. The Rabbi became silent.

A bunch of youths came running toward the Alter down the main corridor. Two others remained at the door to prevent escape. They looked ominous.

"Hand over your money!" they demanded. "We know you got plenty of it," they added. Precious Torah scrolls were thrown to the ground. Silver cups were pocketed. Prayer books were torn.

Most of the congregation stood motionless, except for the Holocaust Survivors who hurriedly rushed to the door. They had seen horrifying scenes like this before. I grabbed the seat in front of me and readied to join others in pouncing on these scumbags. Certainly someone has called for the police. But there was to be no rebellion. Instead, the Rabbi calmly explained that no one has anything worthy of stealing since it is not permitted to carry money on the holiday.

Men whispered in small groups as the Rabbi tried to negotiate some sort of arrangement with these scoundrels. "Let the Rabbi handle this. He has experience with these types," someone said, when there was pressure to act decisively. Another wondered why there weren't guards at the door. No one thought it a good idea to call the police. "Why should they care? They are all anti-Semites," they alleged.

Eventually the mob left. Five Thousand dollars, I heard, was agreed to be ready for payment next week before Yom Kippur services. Fighting them will make things worse they reasoned. They could come back and burn the synagogue down like they did in Brooklyn. People might get attacked on the way to services. Many were pleased at the practical way in which this affair was defused. I was distraught.

Dave listened intently to the description of this unfortunate affair the following evening. He asked details about their appearance and their numbers. What colour were they? Did they wear black leather jackets with a dragon drawn on the back? How many were they? Did they wear red Converse sneakers? He seemed to know who they were.

Gang loyalty was important to Dave. He had promised protection and would keep his word. "Five Thousand bucks!" he exclaimed. "I can do it for less, "he eagerly promised.

"What's that?" I asked.

"Don't worry, I'll take care of this," he ensured.

"But, what about gang loyalty… the promise… the self-defence?" I argued.

"Bull Shiit, Man!" he replied. "Five Thousand bucks is Five Thousand bucks."

VIII

My trusted German Shepard dog, Sabra, knew more about loyalty than Dave did. Sabra's allegiance to me was unconditional. He devoutly remained at my side while walking through dark turns in the park. His ears perked attentively to subtle hints of need. I had no doubt that Sabra would unreservedly endanger himself to protect me from peril, as long as it didn't compete with his innate, irresistible allure to a fresh piece of meat or a bitch in heat.

In many ways Sabra was my best friend. He anxiously awaited my safe return home and tirelessly craved my affection. Sabra liked to play rough, as I did, but never did I fear harm – although he could bite the head off of a venomous Cobra if challenged. He comforted me in times of sorrow, amused me when I was bored, and needed me when others thought I was useless.

We asked nothing of each other, but loyalty.

School continued its steadfast preparation for the upcoming college entrance exams, next year. Most students began to buckle down and formulate a direction for their future. For some guidance was offered about post-graduate careers. Others attuned their efforts in favour of academic pursuits, or scholarship opportunities. The adult world was just around the corner. The only problem was that I was facing the other way.

Despite my best efforts, Dave's inclusion into my life was beginning to take a toll. I soon found myself cutting classes, or misbehaving in them. Exams were failed and homework was ignored. Mrs. O'Neil, my Social Studies teacher, promptly excluded me from class after provocatively comparing her perfume to the smell of cheap whiskey. The same occurred in biology lab for misusing the microscope to examine a specimen of fresh semen.

Inevitably I was called to stand before the Dean after an unfortunate incident in English class during which a board eraser was thrown through the glass pane window above the door. He was surprised to see me under these circumstances. Usually our conversations concerned articles for the school newspaper, which I edited, or the organisation of various community events. He wondered what had happened to me. All I could do was to muster an obnoxious smirk and maintain that he had no solid proof of my guilt. He stared at my Arista badge - struggling with the urge to rip it off my chest. I, almost, wished that he had.

I sought refuge in activities that did not include Dave, the school, or the neighbourhood. The classified section at the back of the Village Voice newspaper provided many alluring opportunities to reclaim my self worth. One advertisement promised easy profits by *Selling Wild Flowers at Wild Hours.* This placed me at the corner of Columbus Circle in Manhattan at one in the morning with a basket of colourful, acrylic flowers, which I sold for one dollar.

Next I volunteered to participate in a psychology research study at Columbia University. It had something to do with gender bias.

The ingenious research design, which led me to believe that marketing skills were being investigated, impressed me. I took home ten bucks for my participation and the promising idea that this might be interesting to do when I grow up.

I attended free introductory lectures about Scientology, Hare Krishna, and the Moon's Unification Church. Avid disciples flogged their panacea for success and tranquillity like one would sell a used car. It frequently involved some sort of audience participation in which we were directed to face the stranger sitting next to us and 'get in touch' with something. Many had a peculiar, hypnotic look in their eyes, as if entranced by a sudden enlightened notion that only they realised. The weirder they looked, the more normal I felt.

At the headquarters of the Jewish Defense League (J.D.L.) on 34th Street, I joined an energetic group of peers busily preparing placards for a public demonstration demanding freedom for our oppressed Jewish brethren in Russia. We sat in protest to block the busy traffic on the Avenue of the Americas, near the USSR embassy. Police firmly tapped us on the shoulder and read out a statement explaining that we were in breach of a particular public ordinance, and that we would be arrested if we did not voluntarily escort them to the sidewalk. There was little resistance from most of the protestors, except for a small group of red-helmeted zealots, whom I recognised from an earlier protest against the Vietnam War.

For some the proliferation of public protest offered the opportunity to be heard. It became a popular pastime for others. There were so many political rallies in the 60's that a dedicated segment was provided at the end of the television news broadcast in which a list of 'TOMORROWS DEMO'S' was screened somewhere between the weather report and the sombre scroll of Vietnam War casualties.

As a JDL activist I managed to slip into the restricted area during a visit to the United Nations. I casually followed a group of VIP guests through a secure entrance and into a plush lounge in which distinguished diplomats were determining world affairs under the liberating influence of a double martini. The General Assembly Auditorium was vacant in readiness for an upcoming meeting. There I hurriedly scribbled a derogatory remark on the second page of the notepad at the desk of the USSR ambassador before running out.

Eventually I was introduced to the outspoken leader of the JDL, Rabbi Meir Kahane (R.I.P.). I told him about the incident with the Synagogue raiders. Kahane silently tightened his lips and gently nodded in recognition of a familiar plight. I had hoped that he would mobilise an army of tough guys to stand guard in the beleaguered community. After a few moments of silence, Kahane stammered, "So, where is your father? Why hasn't he come, as well?" He looked angry, embittered, and tired. My leader he would not be.

My stimulating plunge into the greater arena opened a world of alluring opportunities. But mostly it illuminated a collection of embittered, misguided, and strange characters desperately searching for meaning, like me. I was not particularly impressed. My only option was to resolve the pending issue with Dave, whom I had conveniently blamed for my predicament. The way forward would present itself in time if I remained patient and astute.

Dave was beginning to lose patience with my increasing dissociation from gang life. He listened to explanations of my absences with a tightening of the lips and gentle nod, in a similar way that Kahane had done. I knew that it would be a matter of time before Dave placed me among the growing number of people who have, in his eyes, betrayed him. This wasn't going to end well.

Suddenly Dave enticed me back into his world with an irresistible invitation to see *The Doors* in concert. He, of course, had a cousin who worked as a stagehand and could easily get us in. We met Julio in the early evening. He could drive and had access to his father's station wagon that could pack all eight of us. The concert venue was somewhere in the countryside, just out of the city limits.

Upon arriving, there was a large crowd of impatient fans pressing hard on the locked doors of the auditorium. It was dark, raining, and cold. Dave, however, rapped a code on to the stage entrance door. It was opened from within. We taunted the unfortunate concert hopefuls through the glass doors of the main entrance.

One hour after the scheduled start time the doors were finally opened. We hurriedly staked out an advantageous standing position near the stage, which we vigorously secured.

Another half hour went by and still no music. The mob was getting understandably restless. Eventually a nervous-looking executive entered the stage with a microphone. He announced that *The Doors* had cancelled due to the inclement weather. We would, however, be offered a full performance by their back up band, *The Electric Fudge*. This didn't go down well. Things got nasty. I looked toward the exit.

The atmosphere was totally different at a five-day music festival, Woodstock, several months earlier. Nobody seemed particularly concerned about mundane practicalities, like who was performing. The stage became virtually coincidental. It was dwarfed by the real show, which was in the crowd. Those who did not come to Woodstock to get away from the world sought a way to be a part of it.

Woodstock defied logic. Peace-loving Hippies and Hell's Angels danced to the same rhythm. Nature lovers raved at the exquisite electric guitar solos of Jimmy Hendrix. Health gurus tripped on red, or blue, pills that were passed around, while political activists shared food with undercover F.B.I. agents. It was easy to expect explosive friction in this intense mixture of opposites, but tranquillity managed to paradoxically coincide with loud music. No doubt drugs had something to do with the unique aura at Woodstock. The Woodstock Happening was to become the icon of a generation whose favourite statement about it would simply be, "If you recall being there, then you weren't."

Electric Fudge, alas, were not to be so fortunate. Despite the background roar of an angry audience they began to retune their instruments. The drummer unwisely kicked his foot 'accidentally' into his base drum. No matter, they said, our lead guitarist will play his rendition of a favourite tune. He produced an electrified version of the theme song to a popular comedy television programme, *The Beverly Hillbillies.* The crowd exploded.

The next thing that happened proved that the band had to be drunk, or otherwise stoned on drugs. The lead guitarist produced a hand-held fire extinguisher from back stage. "You've got to cool down," he announced, as he elatedly sprayed us with white foam. A full-scaled riot ensued. Empty beer bottles were flying everywhere, chairs were smashed, and people got trampled upon. I skilfully manoeuvred a path to the exit and waited for the others near the station wagon. Dave arrived much later with scraped knuckles and splattered blood on his shirt. He was absolutely thrilled. I had never seen him so happy.

All had made it to the car, except our driver, Julio. He eventually arrived with something under his trench coat. "Let's get the hell out of here," he commanded. Julio saw that irate rioters had stormed the stage. They were smashing everything. Julio, an avid guitarist, decided to save the Les Paul electric guitar that was mercilessly abandoned on stage. He would make good use of it.

Several days later we visited Julio at his apartment. Dave brought a large amplifier, which had conveniently fallen off a truck at yet another cousin's shop on 42nd Street. Julio excitedly produced the purple, crescent-shaped guitar that was securely hidden in a locked closet. He gently removed a protective blanket and plugged the guitar into the amp. Julio methodically picked various chords commenting on the superb quality in tone and pitch. He skilfully played the infamous rendition of *The Beverly Hillbillies,* from memory. We laughed. His repertoire was extensive. I enjoyed this more than *The Doors* concert that never was.

Dave was surprised at Julio's talent. He didn't know that Julio played the guitar, at all. "How is it that your friends don't know you can play so well?" I asked, wondering why it was kept secret. Julio quietly explained that Dave feels threatened by the success of others. It makes him feel inadequate. To Dave you are either far below him, or out of his reach. There is no middle ground, he explained. This sounded familiar. Dave's world is defined by power, not loyalty - as I had mistakenly assumed. It is power that motivates him. I must find a way to manipulate Dave into distancing himself from me and not the other way around.

IX

I envisaged that it would be like taking candy from a baby. Offer him a shiny, noisy rattle and the baby is in a dilemma beyond that which his rudimentary cognitive abilities can unravel. Invariably the candy is dropped in order to grab the new, enticing toy. In that way there is no crying, no protest, and no violent temper tantrums. Simple! I just needed to find a suitable rattle for Dave.

I had to spend time with Dave, alone, in order to probe his hidden psyche. Away from the protective influence of the gang, Dave was likely to be more spontaneous - less guarded. Unaware, Dave would provide me with the missing key to his confounding behaviour.

We went for long walks in the dark park at night when there was nothing to distract Dave's attention but his own thoughts. He disclosed revealing details about his complex past. The crucial information was embedded in what he didn't say, more than what he did. He didn't like talking about his father, who was described in damming terms as an oppressive authoritarian. I knew this was a sensitive issue for him.

Dave spoke ambivalently about his father, who ruled the family with an iron fist and a can of beer. Dave feared him, yet longed for his approval. There was a time when Dave absolutely adored his father. He cherished him. He admired him. There was mutual respect. Something cracked during Dave's adolescence. Violent rows erupted as the children sought independence. Rules became more rigid, rather than accommodating. Gradually Dave saw less and less of his dear father. He would arrive home late in the evening, usually drunk and demanding. The fall from grace was devastating for Dave. He began to see his father as a broken man who feebly attempted to maintain his status by inertia rather than merit. Dave felt betrayed by him.

At home Dave quickly became self-reliant in a disordered world governed by rules of survival more than family nurturance. He was the only son, born after six girls. Nobody ensured that his needs were met. If you weren't quick at the dinner table you went hungry. As the youngest Dave rarely got to watch his favourite programmes on television, sleep in his own bed, use the bathroom when needed, or ensure his privacy. Things only changed as he matured. Dave was no match for his sisters' quick tongue and subtle manipulations, but his superior physical strength prevailed.

This is what Dave concluded about life. "It's a dog-eat-dog world," he would say. To Dave everything became a struggle for survival – even, existence. Either you exert total control or you are devoured. There were no other rules. Approaching him would invariably be viewed with suspicion. "People always want something from you," he concluded. As proof Dave relentlessly tested well-meaning people by behaving provocatively until they lost patience and revealed their 'true' malicious intentions. It was a self-fulfilling prophecy forged by Dave's paranoid mistrust of the world and his perceived sense of vulnerability. The manner in which Dave coped with his insecurity did not resolve his problem, but became his problem. Dave had, quite unwittingly, become the object that he hated the most: his dad.

I invited Dave to escort me to a weekly photography workshop in Manhattan. There, I had arranged free access to a darkroom for processing black and white photographs. I learned helpful techniques such as how to crop and enhance photographs, polarize photos to look psychedelic, and glue prints onto the back of cardboard for wall-displays.

Central Park was my studio. None of my photographs contained people. Most were scenic panoramas, or close-ups of nature. One picture depicted a small lake struggling to keep from freezing over. It evoked nostalgia and loneliness, simultaneously. Another portrayed a solitary Giraffe at the zoo that had decided to feed alone rather than stick with the herd. There were close-ups of an overflowing garbage can, a broken swing in the park playground, and a parking meter that flashed, "Your time has expired." The personal significance of my chosen topics was not immediately apparent to me. As the photograph developed in the darkroom so did its meaning. This unsettled me.

Dave impatiently flipped through my photo album as if looking for something in a mail order catalogue. With each picture Dave proudly announced its content. "That's in the zoo…Here's an old car… That's 57th Street," and so on, like one does when taking an eye examination at the opticians.

"So, what do you think of the pictures?" I asked.

"Yeah. I know them all, but, there is something missing," he replied.

"Missing?" I enquired, defensively.

"Me!" he gleefully replied, " I am missing from your pictures."

Gee, I thought. How obvious? I should have expected that reaction. Of course Dave would struggle to appreciate anything that did not, somehow, include himself. Photographing him may provide the opportunity to study Dave from a different angle as I did with previous objects before the lens. I was more than curious.

I readily gave Dave total autonomy to choose the place, pose, and angle of the shots. Dave elected to pose in a populated area near the fountain in Washington Square so that others could see him being photographed. There had to be action in the pictures, and no close-ups were allowed. He directed me to photograph him from a crouching position so that he would look impressively big. Dave adopted numerous poses, which invariably depicted him as the victor. It was crucial that Dave looked manly in the photographs. His expression was always menacing at the time of exposure, even if it had begun as a smile. He beat his chest in Gorilla fashion and stood over a fallen log as the fearless world explorer Magellan must of done hundreds of years ago. His favourite picture cleverly situated him riding on the back of a ferocious lion made of stone.

As the encoded picture assumed definition on the blank photographic paper, so did my mind. It was clearer than ever. How did I not see this earlier? There was only one place for Dave. Only one place can adequately satisfy his insatiable search for respect and attention. Dave will be among similar minded men who seek domination. He can evoke fear in others, struggle to prove his existence, and exert power over those around him without appearing abnormal. The best thing about this place was its distance from me. There was no alternative. I will have to get Dave into the United States Marines.

X

Gauging Dave's attitude towards the military could not have been easier. War was everywhere in the 1960's. Television news reports of the controversial war in Vietnam were extensive and virtually uncensored. It was the first war to provide live television coverage. War correspondents could hardly suppress their self-satisfied excitement while presenting live, bloody footage of battle; shiny black body bags; and scorching Napalm clouds. Cameras escorted helicopter gun ships in terrifying raids on helpless Vietnamese villagers. Soldiers eagerly provided comment during fortuitous lulls in the battle. Casualty statistics were regularly updated in a manner not dissimilar to the running tally of football league results.

Life on the streets was no less violent. Anti war protestors clashed regularly with National Guard troops at university campuses. A similar battle was seen between civil rights activists and angry racists in reactionary southern towns. Shootouts between gangsters and police were documented, as well. It seemed that everyone had something to fight for as long as there was a camera around.

Hollywood was not far behind with an explosion of violent movies about war, civil strife and life on the streets. Films that sought to promote peace could always be counted on to depict the most graphic scenes of brutality. I suppose that the idea was to shock people into seeking peaceful solutions to their problems. The hero modelled restraint. He did not succumb to aggressive solutions until there was no other option, which was inevitable.

"Oh, the inhumanity of it!" we would say. "How horrible! Did you see how his head was blown off?" I might exclaim. "Let's see it again," someone would suggest. The only theme that was more popular than violence in 60's films was sex, but you had to be seventeen to see the good ones.

Dave's reaction to a turbulent world was predictable. He couldn't understand why it took so long to 'put things right'. Devastated troops returning from the war were pussies, in Dave's eyes. If only he were in Vietnam. He'd show them how it's done. Those Viet Cong Geeks would piss in their pants at the sight of Dave fearlessly charging up a hill with an M-16 in one hand and a RPG in the other. "A-Bomb the mothers!" Dave decreed. Compared to the Bronx… Nam was a stroll in the park.

Whereas countless others nervously scrambled to avoid the military draft, Dave feigned disappointment at being excluded from the action. Conscription for military duty was arbitrarily decided by an ingenious birthday lottery. Three Hundred and Sixty Five tokens, one for each day of the year, were placed in a large barrel, like the one used for bingo. The first date randomly chosen was September 14th. This meant that all eligible men who had the fateful misfortune to be born on this day were conscripted into military duty. Once this was depleted, the second date, April 24th, was called up - and so on. Some frantically evaded service by enrolling for university study, becoming a minister, or wearing pink laced panties to the medical examination. Conscientious objectors were given non-combat post, and a hard time. Some escaped to another country, like Canada, in desperation.

My friend, Harry, had purposefully failed chemistry at university in order to defer graduation, and the draft. He sent off for an instant certificate as an ordained minister in some obscure religious cult in case that wasn't enough. Crazily, Harry surprised us all by enlisting to serve in the Navy after an eventful night for which he had little memory. It had something to do with rejection by a girl and several bottles of Vodka. Harry spent the next four years in a submarine trying to recall her name.

I was lottery-lucky. My birth date, November 19th, was ranked at a comfortable 203. Hence, there was little chance that the eligible men born on the preceding 202 days of the year wouldn't satisfy the hungry belly of the US military. Dave was similarly fortunate, although he didn't admit it. "Bull Shiit, Man! Why should I volunteer to serve with a group of pussies?" was Dave's explanation.

Dave's expressions of bravado didn't wash with me. "You are such a liar!" I accused. "Do you think that war is as easy as it looks in Hollywood?" I added. "Sure you are tough with people weaker than you are. What would you do without the gang behind you? Where would you hide when there are no back alleys? How will you cope under fire?"

At least that is what I wanted to say to Dave, but the only thing to come out of my mouth was, "Yeah, you'll show them!" That is what I said to him the previous week after a regretful incident with the police. It was the first major snowfall of the season. Dave and I perched on a bridge that spanned a major cross-town highway. We foolishly targeted the busy traffic below with snowballs, like a shooting gallery at the fun fair. The best was to see the sudden fright in the drivers' eyes as their windshield was pounded with snow bombs. Suddenly I was powerfully grabbed from behind. Dave, too, was caught around the collar. The irate policeman was red in the face from anger. "What do you think you're doing? You could cause a terrible accident! You doofus idiots!" he charged, as he decided what to do with us.

I cringed in self-disgust. My God, I thought, how stupid of us. Thank goodness we were stopped. I was speechless. Dave, on the other hand, cowered in fear. He begged for mercy. "I am sorry, I am sorry, I am sorry," he pleaded. "Please, don't arrest me. It was his idea," Dave accused, pointing at me.

Eventually we were let go after a stern warning. Dave immediately re-interpreted the incident to fit his preferred self-image. In his eyes I was too frightened to speak. He, on the other hand, had managed to fool the cop into believing him. "What an idiot!" he said.

By the time that we met up with the gang his story had taken on additional details. The burly cop had his hand on his gun, which Dave astutely noticed was ready to fire. There were at least two other cops with shotguns hiding behind the patrol car. Back up help had been summoned. Thanks to his wit and ingenuity we managed to escape before reinforcements arrived. Lucky for me that Dave was around. Lucky for them Dave had kept his cool. "Yeah, you would have shown them!" is all I could say.

Getting Dave to voluntarily enlist into the United States Marine Corps would require more than his affinity for violence. Dave needed to understand how being a Marine would satisfy his needs. More importantly, Dave needed to believe that he could succeed. Only then will Dave be out of my life. Only then can I get on with my future.

Motivating someone to action requires a positive attitude towards it, the understanding that it will satisfy important needs, and that it can be done. This was an important lesson for me. Manipulating Dave will be more complicated than I realised. The other thing that unsettled me was Alex.

Alex and I came to blows after a chance encounter one evening. From a distance, I noticed Alex fixing a car on a dimly lit side street in the neighbourhood. He was with two others. "Hey Alex!" I called out. "Alex, *que passa*?" I yelled. Suddenly Alex dropped his tools and ran off into a dark alley with his two accomplices. Upon approaching the car I saw that it was propped up on four concrete blocks. Three of the wheels had been removed and were lying on the pavement. The headlights were disassembled, as were the side mirrors and the radio. The car was far from being repaired, I realised. It was being stripped. It was not Alex's car but his new leather jacket.

Upon seeing Alex that evening I attempted to apologise for my naïve intrusion into his actions. I got punched sternly in the face. It knocked me down. Alex's vicious assault took me by surprise. He sat on my chest and attempted a second blow, which I blocked. I kneed him in the balls. The gang stood excitedly around us rooting for more. "Pin his arms back!" someone advised Alex. "Bite his ear!" another said to me. They all cheered, "Kick his ass!" We had each other in a headlock, hoping that the other will tire. Eventually Dave intervened. "You wimps! Is that all you can do?" he said.

Alex warned me to stay away from him. "You don't know me and I don't know you outside of the gang!" he said. I was nobody to him. He accused me of distancing Dave from the gang. My intentions were subversive. I was a liar. I was a danger to the gang and shouldn't be trusted. He wasn't fooled.

At first I was appalled by Alex's accusations before realising that this could be my way out of the gang. Indeed, there was no place for both Alex and me in the gang. I was insulted! I had my pride! I had no choice but to leave! My problems were over.

Dave, however, surprised me, yet again, with his lightening quick acute observations. "Bull Shiit, Man! You just jealous!" he said to Alex.

"No, that's alright, Dave. I will leave if I am not wanted," I graciously conceded.

"Bull Shiit, Man! You in my gang for life. We are your family. I trust you and put my life on it," he announced.

Now I was really screwed. I had missed the perfect opportunity to leave the gang behind without appearing to betray Dave.

Everything that Alex said about me was true. He saw right through me from the very beginning. I was neither a friend, nor an ally. But after this incident there was no other option. I could not leave Dave without challenging his public affirmation of my loyalty. I must get Dave to leave me.

Their gang life would come to an end if I had my way. With Dave out of the picture there would be no gang.

XI

My unfortunate encounter with Alex left me devastated. I realised that there was no easy way out of this quagmire. To make matters worse, Dave began demanding more attention from me in order to cement an illusory bond between us. If only he had heeded Alex's warning? If only I had the guts to confirm Alex's suspicions of me? If only I had a good friend like Alex on my side?

My friends had summarily distanced themselves from me. I was carefully avoided in school, blatantly shunned in public, and coldly excluded from their lives. No one had realised my predicament and stood up for me, as Alex did for Dave. It was a betrayal. I felt abandoned.

I decided to approach them after an uneasy silence during Gym class. I found them at the far side of the locker room, jokingly teasing each other about their smelly sports uniforms.

"Hey Guys!" I called, "What about my gym shorts? I haven't washed them for two years," I proudly proclaimed, as I comically attempted to prop the stiff shorts upright on the wooden bench between us. Normally this would have elicited a conciliatory remark, or a competitive challenge. Even a teasingly endearing insult would do. Gary, I noticed, struggled to suppress a giggle. But the others were less forthcoming.

"Yeah, Dave, you stink!" is what they callously said. It wasn't funny.

The conversation got serious. I confronted them with their unjust abandonment of me. The entire, sad, predicament with Dave was explained. I told them about Dave's unyielding demands for attention, his hypersensitivity to betrayal, and my fateful confrontation with Alex. I would have expected good friends to voice concern rather than admonishment. Instead of support I got alienation. Despite concerted efforts to appear calm and resolute, my voice betrayed a revealing quiver. Angry words lagged frustratingly behind an accusatory finger, like a poorly dubbed foreign language flick. Fortunately I neither stammered nor cried.

I reminded them of our success in the community baseball play-offs last year. Then there was the incident when Scott's mom was taken to the hospital, and I was there. What about the time that we found a hidden stash of vintage Playboy magazines in Mr. Warren's physics lab, and the secret pact we made to arrange for a hooker to visit the hospital if one of us was on his deathbed, and still a virgin? Was this not worth something? Surely they can empathise with my difficulty and help me out.

They surprisingly offered little sympathy for me - other than to listen attentively to my tirade. It was I, in their eyes, who had abandoned them in favour of Dave. He was trouble and so was I, as long as he continued to control me. A slap in the face would have hurt less.

"He doesn't control me," I angrily contested.

"Yeah sure," they cynically replied. "It certainly doesn't look that way," they argued.

I assured them of my ability to manipulate Dave, but they were not convinced. "Show us," they challenged.

"Okay, on Monday you will have proof that Dave is like putty in my hands," I nervously predicted.

The following weekend was spent racking my brains to find a way of convincing my friends that Dave was manageable. I desperately needed to come up with a way that will prove, beyond the shadow of a doubt, that I was in control. It was as important to my friends as it was to me.

At Monday lunch break I squeezed into a vacant seat among my jury of friends. They asked about Dave. "You'll see," I replied. "Dave will be here soon. You will have all the proof you need," I promised.

All eyes were on Dave as he entered the dining hall. They stared in astonishment as he casually signalled me to join him at our regular table near the window. Dave was dressed in his usual combat gear. However, his head was cleanly shaven, except for a residual mane of black hair running down his scalp. It was a Mohawk. He, also, had a large gold ring pierced into his left ear. The look was ridiculous, yet frightening.

"So, what do you think now?" I proudly asked. "I got him to do a Mohawk. The ring was his idea," I explained.

"You did that?" they asked, buckling in laughter.

I told them about my elaborate plan. Dave would do anything if he thought it would gain him respect. He yearned for people to fear him. He craved attention. Knowing this, I had cunningly taken Dave to see an old Western flick in which cowboys fought savage Indian warriors. The Mohawk, I explained, was universally seen as a symbol of courage. Only the bravest warriors were permitted to scalp their heads in this fashion. Everyone immediately recognised someone with a Mohawk as a person of valour and respect. He is singled out of the crowd. Indeed, it takes guts to do it, I added. The rest was easy.

Dave remained blissfully unaware of how ludicrous he looked. "See, everyone is staring at me. Look how they are afraid of me. Wouldn't it be great if the rest of the gang did this?" he excitedly exclaimed.

"Yeah, but it is only the chief who gets to wear a Mohawk. That way everyone will know you are the leader," I contrived.

Dave thought this sounded logical. He thanked me for the brilliant idea and said that Alex would never have thought of this. I hastily agreed. Dave wondered if waxing the Mohawk would make it more prominent. I thought it was noticeable enough. He asked why I was not eating my sandwich. I explained that I was suddenly not hungry.

Indeed, it was the first time that I felt sorry for Dave. My devious power over him overwhelmed me. I had proven myself to old friends at Dave's expense, but hardly felt worthy of their friendship. Perhaps, I hoped, there was another way.

Two subsequent events convinced me otherwise. The first came in the form of a novice school guidance counsellor. She had called me into her office to discuss my disappointing performance on the mock college entrance exams. The Preliminary Scholastic Aptitude Tests (PSATs) provided a predictive score in Maths and English prior to the real examination, next year. Colleges largely relied on these scores in determining suitability for admission. The other factors considered were school grades, results on the Regents Matriculation Examination, two letters of reference, and the fortuitous categorisation as a member of an ethnic minority, from which Jews were strangely excluded.

She noticed that I had indicated an interest in studying veterinary medicine at the prestigious Cornell University, which was out-of-state. Their reputation for academic excellence was exemplified by Cornell's claim to have made dramatic advances in cow-breeding techniques, which gave them the nickname, 'MOO-U'. It, also, meant that they had the best ice cream ever.

Out of the limited spaces for new admissions, one half was restricted to local residents. Most of the remaining offers were extended to members of under-represented minority groups and women. This meant that I would essentially be competing with thousands of hopeful applicants for the 2-3 places left. " With your score, you'll be lucky to receive the automatic post card notification that your application was being processed," jibed the counsellor. "How about a training programme in auto mechanics?" she consoled.

I was in shock. My good friends will undoubtedly go on to experience an adventurous life at university, while I will remain stuck in a Bronx cesspool. My parents will neither love me nor feed me anymore. Eventually I might find a regular night job stripping stolen cars in a seedy garage under my tiny apartment near the elevated subway on Jerome Avenue. My hard earned wages will pay for the chocolate addiction of my fat, wart-nosed wife, who will bear eight closely aged children, whose names will begin with the letter 'Z'. I looked for an opened window.

I tried to explain that I had hardly prepared for the exam. It did not reflect my actual potential, and I would do much better next year. The counsellor was certain that I would try my best, but scores are fairly consistent, within a range of 6-8 percent. "How about an apprenticeship in carpentry?" she excitedly suggested. "I noticed that you received a special commendation from the woodworking instructor after making a beautiful corner shelf. Certainly, your Mom was happy with that," she placated.

"Yeah, my parents would be happy with anything I chose to do with my life as long as it required a 'DR' before my name," I angrily replied, as I stormed out of her office. What an idiot, I thought? How dare she determine my future on the basis of one exam? Counsellor? My ass!

Of course she wasn't aware of the incident in which Dave used my PSAT revision book to feed a barrel-fire on a cold winter evening in the park. She wasn't around when the gang got me excluded from the public library for tearing photographs of bare-chested Peruvian natives out of the National Geographic Magazine. How could she understand the difficulty concentrating after a sleepless night due to the excitement of being chased by the police for spraying graffiti on subway trains?
She didn't know any of these things, because I didn't tell her.

The other thing that happened sealed Dave's fate for good. It came to mind every time I began to feel sorry for him. In a strange way it gave me the strength to follow through with my plan, and to rid myself of Dave for good. Oddly it occurred the same day that my dreams were smashed.

The inexperienced guidance counsellor had unwittingly done more good than she realised. Her feeble attempts to soften the blow made me realise how vulnerable and miserable I appeared. My dire situation was severe and would require some serious thinking. I had not the energy to continue with classes that day. The park was across the street. There, in a small clearing, I came across the gang who were laughing and joking as they stood in a circle. Despite my deep reservations about the gang, I didn't want to be alone.

Upon approaching I noticed Dave standing in the middle of the gang. He was energetically swinging a long rope above his head, as a rustler would do in order to lasso a wild steer. A dark weight was tied to the end so that it made a *swishing* sound as it picked up orbital speed. Dave positioned himself at a particular distance from a large Oak tree, nearby. He carefully swung the rope so that the tied weight would barely scrape by the tree. Occasionally he would miscalculate, causing the weight to thud into the tree's massive trunk. It was then that I noticed the cat. Its tail was wired onto the rope's end. It was barely alive.

My complaints were met with outrageous slurs of laughter. "It's a fuck'n *Gato,* Man! What you so excited about?" they jeered. All I could do was to frown disgust. Every revolution of the cat was like winding a watch to supply power to my convictions. Each 'thud' nailed a vital step into my plot. By the time that the cat was finally dead, my plan was alive and clawing its way out of my ambivalence. Dave would soon be out of my life. The gang will cease to exist. I will go on to university. The cat will be revenged, and world order will be restored.

XII

The first thing on my agenda was to accumulate information about military enlistment. This was easy enough. A thick packet of colourful brochures promptly arrived in the mail following a brief enquiry at the local Marine Recruitment Center. My inquisitive parents understandably voiced concern upon arrival of the material that was clearly labelled '**FIRST TO GO IN, LAST TO LEAVE: THE MARINES**'. I explained that I was preparing for an important project, which was crucial towards my plans for further education. This wasn't far from the truth.

The covering letter was addressed to me. It congratulated me on my noble intention to come to the aid of my country in time of need. Patriotic Americans stood up for their country, the flag, and righteous values. As a Marine I would be joining a proud legacy of courageous fighters who were revered at home and abroad. As if that wasn't enough, enlisting in the Marines promised me a decent salary, extensive educational and career training, a comprehensive health care plan, and a sizeable pension. No mention was made of Vietnam, except for the alluring opportunity to, "see the world." The Marine learns to focus on the important things in life, while the non-essential is discarded, which is exactly what I did with the letter.

The brochures, however, were very useful. They included large colourful photographs of recruits energetically climbing a balsam rope in basic training. There were pictures of soldiers cueing up to receive a hearty meal in the canteen, a contented platoon standing in formation, a basketball game, and uniformed soldiers casually watching a film in the camp's modern cinema. A four-star holiday in an exclusive country club was nothing compared to the adventurous experiences in the Paris Island boot camp.

Dave needed to picture himself in these scenes. To accomplish this I cut out pictures of Dave's face from photographs and meticulously pasted them onto the heads of promising figures in the brochure so that Dave could see himself jumping fearlessly from an airplane, leading a platoon on a 6-mile hike, and receiving a medal for bravery from a busty celebrity.

Most of the gang found my creative alterations amusing. Dave, however, became pensively silent. I could sense that the seed, which I had deviously planted, was taking root.

"You gotta be tough to get through Marine training," I remarked aloud.

"Bull Shiit, Man. I could do it blindfolded," he predicatively claimed.

We created a makeshift training course in the vestigial back alley behind the Laundromat. Eight discarded tyres were laid on the pavement in two columns of four. You had to hop through the central rings of the wheels in order to reach the next obstacle, which consisted of two rows of garbage cans. After vaulting over those you had to swing over a pit of broken glass using an old telephone cable. Finally, a high chain-linked fence needed to be scaled. Later, important improvements were added to include a comically dressed dummy, which was stuffed with old newspapers, that required stabbing, and several precarious leaps between the rooftops of adjacent buildings. The entire obstacle course could be completed within 12.5 minutes, if you were good. Conveniently, Mr. Cunningham had misplaced his stopwatch during Gym class. With this I kept a careful record of scores during our regular competitions. I ensured Dave's prowess by delaying onset of the timer until he was clear of the first obstacle. I purposefully achieved the slowest scores among the gang.

"Don't worry," consoled Dave, "You gotta be tough like me to be a Marine," he explained. I asked for his advice in order to improve my disappointing performance, which he eagerly offered.

One evening, four sailors happened to barge into Gino's while Mercedes and I were paying for the Pizza. We were rudely shoved aside as they approached the counter asking for four family sized pizzas. "Sorry, we've been celebrating in the bar across the street," apologised the one closer to me, "Drunk as a skunk, we are."

"Came back from Nam?" I guessed.

"Na, ain't been there yet," he explained. The last three months were spent stalking a Russian submarine somewhere in the Indian Ocean, or, were the Russians stalking them? They weren't exactly sure. But they did know the words to a drinking song that contained one sentence,

"The Navy gets the gravy, and the Army gets the beans. Beans, Beans, Beans, Beans..."

"So, what was the party about?" I asked.

They explained that Jimmy, who was leaning over the counter, had won a Dolphin Pin. The official way to achieve this coveted badge was to demonstrate complete mastery over whatever device you are responsible for, like a radar oscilloscope. However the more popular way to get a dolphin pin was to challenge someone with it to a dare in any land-based bar. If the dare is accepted, one half pitcher of beer is presented to the challenger. The others fill the remaining half pitcher with any drink available at the bar. In Jimmy's case this included two shots of vodka, one glass of Tequila, a few glasses of cheap wine, and a tablespoon of chocolate milk with Tabasco sauce. The prized dolphin pin is dropped into the concoction. Jimmy successfully managed to drink the entire pitcher in one go and catch the pin between his teeth, before vomiting his guts out. Now, they were hungry.

Mercedes whispered a request for me to ask them about their uniforms, which clearly impressed her. She wondered if they had ever killed anyone. What do their girlfriends do while they are in a submarine for three months, she asked? They thought that a photograph of her on their locker would make the time go by faster. Mercedes blushed.

Upon returning to the back table we found Dave green with envy. He turned his back on Mercedes. "Who do they think they are?" he contested.

"Hey, don't take it out on Mercedes," I remarked, "She cannot help it. All women have a thing for Men in uniform," I provocatively consoled.

Dave wound himself up with anger. "These punks need to be taught a lesson," he decreed. A plan was devised to ambush them as they left Gino's in much the same way as was done to me several months ago.

I managed to slip a caution note to the doomed submariners as we stormed out of the shop. I hoped that they were sober enough to take heed of my warning. Indeed, after several minutes we discovered that they had stumbled through the back door of the shop and disappeared, averting a disaster and preventing Dave from demonstrating his worth in Mercedes' eyes.

"So, those fuckers are scared of me," Dave proudly proclaimed, as he pounded his chest. "Army, my ass!" he exclaimed.

"No, they were Navy," corrected Mercedes.

"Army, Navy, same bull shiit," concluded Dave. He was just as tough as they were. He still had something to prove.

The final element in my plan arrived by chance. The school had invited the military recruitment team to speak before the general assembly. The presentation was well organised and impressive. There were colour slides, a display of weapons and protective vests, a demonstration of hand-to-hand combat, and some inspiring talks by three proud recruits who had made the transition from the dead end neighbourhood to a fulfilling military career. Following the talk I asked Dave to escort me towards the stage so that I could speak to one of the representatives. We approached a tall Marine who was distributing leaflets to other students. I was deemed to young to enlist.

"What about you?" he asked looking at Dave. "You look old enough. You are exactly the kind of Man that the Marines need," he said.

Dave's response was unremarkably, "Bull Shiit."

"Yeah, well, take this Bull Shit and give me a call. Here's my number," the unflustered Marine said while handing Dave a leaflet.

It was a gift from heaven. I could not have staged something more perfect. Dave shoved the material into his back pocket without saying a word. I, too, kept silent. He mentioned nothing of this interchange to the gang. The more he kept this to himself the more important it was to him. That was Dave's way of dealing with personal issues. The rest was for show.

It didn't take long for Dave to disappear from the scene. He didn't say a word about his intentions. Suddenly he was gone. I wasn't sure if Dave was gone forever, or on one of his mysterious 'business trips', as he would call them. Despite my curiosity I didn't approach the gang to ask – in case they would confirm my fears.

Days turned into weeks, and weeks into months. I quickly reclaimed a comfortable place at school and with friends. The top grade was achieved for a class History project, called Cop Out, which described the government's acquiescence concerning harrowing reports of concentration camps during World War II. Comparable achievements were achieved in Spanish and English. In the biology laboratory I became known as the expert in painlessly anaesthetising frogs. The class production of *Oklahoma* went superbly well, even though I had sung my lines. Friends commented on my impatient thrust into school activities. They wondered if I was trying to make up for lost time during my episode with Dave. The truth, however, was less positive. I felt that I needed to make the most of my liberty before Dave returns. For this eventuality I had no plan.

Two months later Dave walked into the Dining Hall. Again everyone stared at him as he scanned the tables in search of me. He was in full military uniform. His head was neatly shaven, and his boots were meticulously shined. He looked impressive.

"So, what do you think?" he asked, "How do I look?"

"You look great, Dave," I replied. This time I wasn't lying.

Dave invited me to join him for lunch outside of the school. We picked up some tasty snacks at the local grocery. Surprisingly Dave offered to pay. The owner, however, refused to take his money, as a gesture of respect. Dave told me about his experiences in Marine boot camp as we went for a leisurely walk in the park. Sure the training was tough, but so was he. Other recruits couldn't stop crying for their momma, he reported. Dave was the best marksman, undefeated in hand-to-hand combat, and led the unit to victory in mock war games. His commanding officer had tried to boss him around, but Dave put him straight. I didn't care how much of this was true. It was what I wanted to hear. It was what Dave wanted me to believe.

Prior to leaving Dave pulled out a letter from his back pocket. It was notification of transfer to Vietnam. "I owe this all to you," he remarked. Surprisingly, he didn't sound angry. I was relieved.

That was the last time that I saw Dave. I was never to hear from him again. News reports about the intense situation in Vietnam worried me. Within a few years the war would be over. A final, desperate attempt to win a decisive victory led to fierce face-to-face battles and many casualties, before the political will to endure was lost. I looked for mention of Dave in the daily news reports of American casualties. However, I suddenly realised that I never bothered to learn Dave's surname. Scanning the casualty lists for someone called Dave from the Bronx, New York was ridiculously random. I had no choice but to ask the gang, whom I have avoided since Dave's sudden departure.

The Laundromat was full of busy customers stuffing clothes into washing machines, pulling steamy linen from industrial dryers, and impatiently waiting for the completion of a particular cycle. The gang was not to be found, except for Alex, who was crouching down next to the exposed turbine of an antiquated clothes dryer.

"Alex, *que passa*?" I asked.

He looked up, briefly, and flatly said, "Hey Jew, what you want?" while unintentionally pointing a large screwdriver at me. Alex explained that he had taken on the job as manager of the Laundromat after the Chinese woman slipped on a bar of soap and broke her back. He was very busy and didn't have time for me. As the manager, Alex prohibited the gang from using the Laundromat as their hangout - it was bad for business. He hadn't heard from Dave, either.

I asked about Dave's family name. Alex replied, "It is *punyo*. That is it, Dave *DePunyo*," he confirmed. I left without shaking his hand. The feeling was mutual. I soon discovered that Alex was lying to me. *DePunyo* was not Dave's real surname, but it was a derogatory term, in Spanish, that Alex would never dare say directly to Dave - without expecting to be killed. I decided to stop my anxious search for news about Dave. It was time to let go and to get on with my life.

Meanwhile my personal plans progressed nicely. I managed to receive a scholarship to university, and chose a small college in South Carolina. It was as far away from the Bronx as I could imagine. Shortly afterwards my family joined me to live in the comfortable community of Charleston. There, people lived in nice, large houses with a garden in the front and back. Many families had at least two cars. Some went fish'n regularly and marched in parades during state holidays. People like me could easily enjoy a quality of life that I thought existed only on television. My heavy Bronx accent quickly disappeared. I joined a college fraternity from whom I needed to keep few secrets. Friends invited me to their homes for dinner and introduced me to their neighbours. I received a double Bachelor's Degree of Science in Biology and Psychology. Later I continued graduate studies in Clinical Psychology. My experiences growing up in the Bronx became comfortably distant, but never went away, entirely.

What about Dave, I wondered? He was very likely killed in Nam, or worse. I feared that Dave could be disabled in a wheelchair, hooked on heroine, and cursing the day that he ever met me. Unsettling thoughts of my underhanded manipulation of Dave continued to haunt me, on occasion. At these times I summoned memories of the wretched cat as it was swung mercilessly into a tree, the relentless beating of Dave's cousin and the photographer, and Dave's stubborn intrusion into my life. Nonetheless, I often thought what I would say to Dave if he suddenly reappeared. I could apologise for the way that it was I, in the end, who bullied him. I could explain the reasons for my rejection of his friendship. Then again, I might simply say,

"Bull Shiit, Man! That'll teach you for woof'n on me!"

EPILOGUE

I have not stepped foot into the Bronx since 1971. Infrequent visits to New York City are restricted to Manhattan, for the most part. I maintain that there is plenty to do and see in Manhattan when my son wants to see where I grew up. "The Bronx has nothing to offer, except for a slum of burned out buildings and the Yankee's baseball stadium," I explain. Alas, total exclusion of the Bronx from my thoughts is hardly absolute. It comes to mind when facing similar characters, like Dave, in my clinical practice. Identifying ways to motivate patients to adopt healthy behaviours are based, in part, on lessons learned while manipulating Dave to enlist into the Marines. My clinical experience in the treatment of Holocaust Survivors reinforces important principles that I have learned about resilience and coping in difficult conditions. The significance of the community in providing support for the vulnerable comes to mind when providing for the chronically ill. Finally, my Bronx experience has imprinted important lessons about the vital, albeit uncomfortably slight, distinction between caring for others and exploiting them.

These are the issues that I would like to discuss in the Epilogue of *Shrink*. My fateful experience in the Bronx had taught me many things about myself, the psychology of people, and society – although I hardly realised this at the time. Subsequent studies in psychology managed to belatedly confirm what I had already known. At the age of 16, however, I acquired an appreciation of the intriguing power of psychology, and its undeniable significance in explaining the dynamics of interpersonal relationships. The following pages will present some pertinent psychological principles in the understanding of relevant **Personality Factors**, the significance of **Motivation**, **Resilience** and **Society**, and a debate about **Ethics**.

PERSONALTIY

Dave was a helluva character, huh? To a large extent, my success in surviving a relationship with someone like Dave depended upon my ability to analyse his needs, predict his reactions to certain events, and understand my significance to his goals in life. Not unlike a laboratory researcher, I observed Dave's reactions to events and staged situations in order to test a particular hypothesis about his personality. Indeed, we are all amateur scientists when faced with the challenge of understanding the curious behaviour of others, especially in ambiguous situations. At times this is deliberate, sometimes subtle. The ability to categorise others into familiar character types comforts us with a perceived sense of mastery and security. Everyone has a tendency to interpret particular events in prescribed ways. Without this there would be no Shakespeare, Michelangelo would hardly be different than Salvador Dali, and Michael Jackson might easily be confused with Mozart. Horror of horrors!

Dave's undeniable personality was exactly that: undeniable. Regardless of how others judged him, he could not be easily ignored. Much of his behaviour had the effect of ensuring his existence in the eyes of others. Threatening situations that exposed an underlying sense of emptiness, or weakness, would invariably evoke a powerful reaction in Dave. His insatiable need for attention screamed, "I am here and cannot be ignored!" Relinquishing control led to inevitable rejection, exploitation, and harm - in Dave's mind. Children, who are faced with a similar existential dilemma, during their developmental years, can react in two opposing ways: to succumb and accept their unimportance, or to rebel and exert relentless control over their world. This vital issue may become prominent in one's psyche to the extent that all situations are based upon it. Everything becomes a struggle for survival. All interpersonal relationships are judged according to one's sense of mastery and security. Nothing is taken for granted. People are not to be trusted, especially if they appear cunningly friendly. This paranoid-like perception of others paradoxically prevents the only situation that may alleviate interpersonal distress: intimacy.

Unfortunately, I have seen many people like this in my clinical practice. Typically they have little problem engaging in relationships. The problems arise when people get to close. That is when the relentless testing of trust occurs. The closer one gets, the more threatening the relationship. Hence relationships are unstable, or unbelievably rigid. People are viewed in extreme terms. You are either good or bad. Figures of supreme authority are absolutely admired until a minor fault is noticed. The fall from grace is as sudden as it is extreme. There is no middle ground.

Most people can identify someone with similar traits. In extreme situations these individuals become criminals or despots, depending on how smart they are. Various therapeutic approaches, ranging from long-term psychodynamic therapy and prescribed cognitive behavioural interventions, have been developed to help similar personalities achieve more stable and constructive lives. The results are not impressive.

MOTIVATION

Knowing does not necessarily equate to doing. How many of us know that smoking is hazardous to our health, yet deny its obvious conclusion? The same is true about the beneficial significance of regular exercise, driving within safe speed limits, revising in advance for exams, and saving for retirement. Awareness about a particular issue, albeit a precursor to change, does not ensure corrective action. It is assumed that one must acquire a proper attitude towards something in order to behave accordingly.

This important principle was clearly illustrated in the elaborate efforts of the United States government to alter the regular eating habits of Americans during World War II. The typical American homemaker protested at the shortage of fresh red meat. Nervous politicians pointed out that plenty of nutritious and tasty meat was available in the form of offal. "Sure, grilled tripe might be good for the culinary oddities of Europe, but Americans eat steak, "they replied. Indeed, in America this valuable source of protein and vitamins was largely reprocessed into dog food. A significant attitude change was necessary in order to establish grilled liver as a staple that normal people eat, unless you are vegetarian. Popular chefs were mobilised to introduce enticing aromatic recipes using goose liver, magazine articles raved at the new, tasty fried intestine hors d'oeuvre at posh dinners, and supermarkets held special introductory sales on chicken gizzards. People ate.

This revealing lesson did not pass unnoticed by a conniving group of American industrialists following the war. Whereas most of the world breathed a sigh of relief upon armistice, a select group of businessmen were distraught. The war had made fortunes for entrepreneurs in the manufacture of jeeps and tanks, oil and steel production, and the rubber tyre industry. They could hardly build enough factories to keep up with the destruction during the war. "What shall we do with our massive enterprise when nothing is getting blown up anymore?" they wondered. Part of their devious solution was the development of the Modern American Automobile. Their engineers were instructed to design a family car that will use as much steel, chrome, rubber, and petrol as possible - without looking too ridiculous. Rear fins were added for show. Extra wide chrome bumpers were secured in front and back. The gas guzzling motor was powerful enough to tug a ship into port, and double thick white-rimmed tyres ensured a superbly comfortable ride.

Who will buy such a monstrosity when war torn Europe had achieved the same in a small, economical car? The attitude experts were called in. An elaborate plan was implemented to convince the typical American man that big means better. Popular celebrities were photographed in a large pink Cadillac, war heroes deserved to live a bountiful life and drive safely through the new tarmac highway system in their chrome bumpered Pontiac convertible, and neighbours will realise how successful you are when a fancy new Chevrolet, with the noticeable fins at the rear, is parked in your suburban driveway. The results of their campaign are obvious for all to see, even today.

So, it seemed that people can be motivated to do just about anything if they have the relevant information, adopt a positive attitude, and perceive the new behaviour as socially acceptable. Subsequent endeavours to discourage racist thinking in the 1960's were not, however, so simple. Stereotypical prejudgements about minorities were challenged, and attitudes towards tolerance were enhanced. Yet the desired change remained elusive. Similar problems were realised in trying to get people to eat five fruits a day, or submit to routine mammography examinations. An undefined factor was missing. Information, attitude and social normalcy contributed to the intention to change, but something else was required in order to actually act.

Subsequent investigations showed that people have to believe in their ability to perform before embarking on new behaviours. It turns out that the more confidence you have in succeeding, the more likely you are to do well. The opposite, alas, is also true. You need the relevant information, a positive attitude, the perception of normalcy, and the belief that you will succeed in order to take that first step and actually get off the sofa and go to the gym.

With Dave I had learned this the hard way. He required little help in developing an affinity, or positive attitude, towards violence. Information about the military was practically unavoidable. My contribution was to ensure that Dave perceived military enlistment as an acceptable act among the people that mattered to him: the gang. Secondly, Dave needed to believe in his ability to enlist in the Marines and to succeed in training. Only then did Dave actually act upon his intention. Only then was my plan realised.

RESILIENCE

I have often wondered whether I 'had what it takes' to survive a Nazi concentration camp. It is a question that one shouldn't have to speculate about. For me, however, it came to mind whenever my parents told me of their harrowing Holocaust experiences. Only recently did I allow myself to address this question openly. Extensive work in providing therapy to Holocaust Survivors helped.

Many survivors appear similarly puzzled by their ability to have endured the atrocities. Some attribute the emergence from the death camps to fate or divine intervention. Others identify a particular Good Samaritan or quick response as their saviour. Most resent the question, as if I were suggesting that they must have done something immoral to prevail, at the expense of others. My own subsequent research into this question has revealed one possible answer: Optimism.

As amazing as it seems, individuals were able to remain optimistic despite the harsh realities of war. Firstly, they did not blame themselves for their sad plight. The reason for their torment was placed firmly on the racist, cruel nature of the camp guards, and not their intrinsic Jewishness, or errors in judgement. Secondly, never did they accept the finality of their situation. The horrible war will eventually end, and so will their suffering. Finally, an optimistic view of their dire situation was enhanced by an adamant adherence to positive self-values, despite the relentless efforts by their tormentors to achieve total domination and to dehumanize them. For instance, the insistence of a female survivor to hold on to a hairbrush as a way of preserving a sense of self-dignity, in denial of the fact that she had no hair, gave her the strength to realise that not all was lost.

Subsequent observations of others, who had coped with adversity, have identified a similar tendency. Having a sense of optimism contributes to the ability to cope, and to survive. Optimists tend to perceive negative events in a similar manner. External forces are responsible for their predicament, not themselves. The situation is time-limited, and therefore transient. Finally, not all aspects of ones life are equally affected by their unfortunate situation. My work with individuals who suffer from chronic pain illustrates this clearly. Difficulties in coping are more pronounced among people who tend to blame themselves for the injury, perceive their pain as permanent, and allow discomfort to disturb all areas of life. The optimist, on the other hand, will realise the importance of external factors responsible for the injury, realistically look forward to regaining a decent quality of life, and maintain important activities, like socializing, despite some difficulties in functioning.

Fortunately my brief Bronx episode was nowhere near to a Holocaust. In fact I do not look back at this period of my life with a sense of trauma, or sadness. It was a situation that was put before me by external forces, for the most part. Somehow I always knew that a resolution would be found. Moreover, important issues were detrimentally affected by Dave, but not all. Problems were not defined as worrying obstacles but thrilling challenges to overcome. Its successful resolution did not leave me traumatised but illuminated a natural interest in psychology.

Recent investigations into the process of ageing reveal even more surprising aspects of survival. People are more resilient than we give them credit for. Money, educational level, and even health are not nearly as important as interpersonal skills. Even more challenging is the discovery that a good social life can help people overcome the most difficult early childhood experiences. Surely a healthy, happy, and nurturing development significantly contributes to long-term happiness. However, people can, under certain conditions, conveniently reprocess and alter past memories in order to fit comfortably into a preferred self-image and enjoy a fruitful and satisfying life in old age.

Only recently have psychologists recognised the curious fact that some people can survive the most appalling conditions more than others. Attention has been refocused on the understanding of resilience, rather than on pathology and risk. What makes one underprivileged child develop into a healthy, good, and constructive citizen when siblings have succumbed to the pervasive environmental influence of drugs, crime, and idleness?

Not only do resilient people survive, they thrive. Overcoming significant tragedy and hardship can leave one feeling traumatised, anxious, and insecure. Amazingly the survivor not only manages to overcome hardship, but also finds a way, in the end, to make the best out of the experience. Indeed, a bereaved wife is likely to feel sad, remorseful, and abandoned. However she can also regain a new appreciation for life and those around her. She may learn to be more independent and discover untapped resources within herself and her surroundings. In other words, if life gives you lemons…make lemonade.

SOCIETY AND ETHICS

Teenagers are like a wet bar of soap. They will slip through our fingers if held too tightly. Conversely, an overly liberal grasp will allow the soap to drop. The developing adolescent requires a certain amount of structure that will serve as a reference point to either adhere to, or to reject. To a large extent, parents and society are responsible for this. My parents clearly expressed their expectations of me, while allowing me the freedom to develop my own way of interpreting this. I knew, as most adolescents do, how my parents would react to certain situations, without having to ask them. I could challenge them, criticize them, and disappoint them without really fearing abandonment. So, when a 15 year old ostracises you for being "so predictable" don't get upset. It is actually a compliment. Know that you are doing well.

Teenagers are particularly vulnerable to external persuasion for physiological reasons, as well. Only in late adolescence is our body fully developed. The final organic structure to develop is the nervous system. It is, also, the first organ to appear in the human foetus. An important element, the myelin sheath, becomes fully formed in the late teens, at the earliest. Individuals who lack this structure, which functions as an isolating coat on the circumference of the nerve cell, tend to think concretely. They lack the ability for abstract reasoning, which allows us to fully comprehend philosophical notions. Hence, the developing adolescent experiences a new understanding of some vital concepts. He, or she, might excitedly approach a member of the older generation with enthusiastic revelations about the meaning of life and society. Too frequently, the callous response of parents is, "Yeah, that is nice, but what about the trash in your room? When are you ever going to clean it?"

During my turbulent developmental phase, the community did not provide me with the vital structure and guidance required while striving to define my identity. They were struggling with their own existential issues. Take, for example, a young adult male growing up in a family that argues. The parents are preoccupied by their own marital issues, and do not attend to his pending needs. What does the teenager do? He may accept a secondary role in life and defer the development of independent reasoning and living. Alternatively, he may look elsewhere for guidance. Any authority that appears to recognise his search for direction, and makes him feel worthy, will do.

People, especially in their youth, demand freedom to establish their own individual direction in life. Yet, too much freedom can become paradoxically oppressing. Modern society has strived to break old restrictive customs that limited personal growth. Arbitrary boundaries for women, gays, and minorities have been broken. Traditional family roles have become more flexible. Nothing will keep you from actualising your potential, but yourself. Shit! How do we choose? Where can we go for guidance? Who do we blame if things don't work out?

Overwhelming opportunities may encourage individuals to look for structure, or a guiding hand. Some are attracted to powerful political figures. A few may turn to dogmatic religious cults. Adopting a superficial existence may defer self-evaluation in others. Active communities that are well organised, and encourage participation, are more likely to provide comfort than apathetic neighbourhoods. Empowered communities have more resources, less crime, are healthier, and promote social responsibility. Worrying contemporary trends, however, suggest that people are less likely to volunteer in their own community. Mobile families may find it easier to relocate than to contribute to the resolution of problems in the neighbourhood. Unprincipled residents, with poorly defined moral codes, rule.

So, why does my experience in the Bronx bother me so much? Why can't I blame society for Dave's fate? How was his decision to enlist into the Marines wrong? Indeed, many served in the armed forces during this period. The government promoted it, society respected it, and Dave wanted it. What is keeping me from considering this episode an adventurous 'coming of age' experience?

The undeniable fact, however, is that Dave's fateful decision to enlist into the military was not his idea - it was mine. The manipulation of Dave was not meant to serve his needs, but mine. Frankly, I didn't give a damn about Dave. My goal was to get him, and the gang, out of my life. Towards this aim I was successful.

The distinction between caring for someone and exploiting them is precariously fragile. The difference, in my view, is based upon needs. Someone is cared for when his, or her, needs are the primary concern. Otherwise, it is exploitation.

Notwithstanding, the results might be identical, if we are lucky. For instance, a wife may provide dedicated care to her ailing husband. Whether the fundamental reason for her concern is based upon his welfare or her financial security does not affect the beneficial value of her actions.

In my case, Dave might have achieved important benefits from military service. He may have received important training, proved heroism in Vietnam, and acquired a sense of self-respect. He was, after all, going nowhere particularly positive in the Bronx. It would have been nice if Dave had reached this conclusion on his own, but he didn't. That makes all the difference.

RECOMMENDED READING

Below is a list of books that I used, directly or indirectly, in preparing the Epilogue of *Shrink*. It is organised according to topical relevance. Some of the references are appropriate for general readership. Others are written for experienced professionals. A brief description of the main subject matter will follow each citing so that you can decide if it is relevant to your interests.

Personality

Winnicott, D.W. (1964). The Child, the Family, and the Outside World. London: Penguin Books.

This classic book is well read by professionals and the general public. David Winnicott presents some astute observations about child development. The topics include Motherhood, Fatherhood, Feeding, Weaning, and Independence. It is available in paperback.

Mahler, M. (1975). The Psychological Birth of the Human Infant: Symbiosis and Individuation. New York: Basic Books.

Margaret Mahler's pioneering theory of Object Relations is illustrated in this classic professional text. Accordingly, the fundamental aspects of personality are hypothesized to have developed from a very early age: before the age of six months. Some intriguing observations of breast-feeding are interpreted and explained. Despite being quite difficult to read, it is worth persevering.

Millon, T. (1969). Modern Psychopathology. Philadelphia, PA: W.G.Saunders Company.

    This professional textbook is written by Theodore Millon, who contributed to the development of the Diagnostic and Statistical Manual (DSM), which is used by psychologists and psychiatrists to determine diagnoses of mental disorders. Millon illustrates the clinical picture, aetiology, and treatment approaches that are relevant to pathological personality disorders. It is my clinical bible.

Greenberger, D., & Pedesky, C.A. (1995). Mind over Mood: Change How You Feel by Changing the Way You Think. New York: Guilford Press.

    Personality trends are convincingly explained in terms of acquired cognitive perceptions about oneself, the environment, and the world. Accordingly, it is hypothesized that people can alter their maladaptive reactions and interpersonal preconceptions by examining and restructuring their cognitive interpretations of events.

Motivation

Bandura, A. (1997). Self-Efficacy: The Exercise of Control. New York: Worth Publications.

    Albert Bandura is a prominent psychological theorist and researcher. This textbook is written for the experienced professional. Self-Efficacy is defined as an "I can do it" attitude. Bandura presents substantial research, which suggests that a positive self- efficacy can predict whether action will be taken, as well as the likelihood of success. A negative sense of self-efficacy has the opposite effect.

Resilience

Seligman, M.E.P., & Buchanan, G.M.(Eds). (1995). <u>Explanatory Style.</u> Hove, England: Lawrence Erlbaum Associates.

    Explanatory Style refers to a basic personality disposition that determines how an individual interprets negative events that befall him, or her. An optimist tends attribute bad events as originating externally, short term, and specific to relevant difficulties. The pessimist, on the other hand, tends to blame himself, or herself; sees the problem as long lasting; and allows the problem to disturb all areas of living. Optimism helps one cope with and withstand hardship.

Wolgroch, D. (2002). "The Effects of Experience on the Explanatory Style of Holocaust Survivors." <u>Doctoral Dissertation Abs.</u> Approved April 2002.

    This is my own empirical research that investigated Explanatory Style among a group of Holocaust Survivors. Using taped interviews of Holocaust Survivors, I extracted references to optimistic or pessimistic interpretations of events. The results suggest that individuals were able to maintain a certain level of optimism during their horrific experiences. I hypothesized that optimism may have aided them in surviving the war.

O'Hanlon,B. (2005). <u>Thriving Through Crises: Turn Tragedy and Trauma into Growth and Change.</u> New York: Perlgee Books.

This inspiring book describes situations in which people were not only able to survive tragedy but went on to extract something enriching and positive out of the experience. It is part of a modern trend in Positive Psychology, which focuses on the development and acquisition of positive coping rather than the examination of pathology and risk. Professionals and the general readership can appreciate this text.

Vaillant, G.E. (2002). Aging Well: Surprising Guideposts to a Happier Life from the Landmark Harvard Study of Adult Development. London: Little Brown and Co.

Although based upon a 66-year empirical study, it is written in a way that can be enjoyed by everyone. This prospective study on ageing studied individuals from the age of 11 to the age of 77. Some of the results challenge popular preconceptions about early development and healthy functioning. Financial status, educational level and health are not nearly as important as the maintenance of quality social contacts. I have recommended this text to many people.

Society and Ethics

Fromm, E. (1969). Escape from Freedom. New York: Henry Holt.

Eric Fromm's groundbreaking book is just as relevant today as in 1969, when it was originally written. Fromm argues that changes in society have deprived people of a sense of security and direction in life. Too much freedom can be overwhelming. Accordingly, Fromm makes some worrying predictions about society and future events.

Putnam, R.D. (2000). <u>Bowling Alone.</u> London: Simon & Schuster.

    Professionals and non-professionals can appreciate this text. Putnam presents substantial evidence, which suggests that society is in a social deficit. Changes in society have led to a lack of community spirit and involvement. Communities that have maintained this collective responsibility have more resources, less crime, better health, and happier residents.

Sanes, D.H., et al. (2006). <u>Development of the Nervous System, 2nd Edition.</u> London: Elsevier Academic Press.

    A professional textbook that describes the contemporary understanding of the nervous system developmental process.

Wesigerber, Karen. (1999). <u>The Traumatic Bond Between the Psychotherapist and Managed Care.</u> London: Jason Aronson Inc.

    This professional text focuses on the effects of the American Managed Care system on the relationship between patient and therapist. To what extent have ethical boundaries been breached in order to comply with managerial, financial, and practice concerns?

Shrink 116